ENCHANTED APRIL

ENCHANTED APRIL

by Matthew Barber

from the novel by Elizabeth von Arnim

JOSEF WEINBERGER PLAYS

LONDON

ENCHANTED APRIL
First published in 2004
by Josef Weinberger Ltd
12-14 Mortimer Street, London, W1T 3JJ

ISBN 0 85676 277 6

Cover artwork design by M Scott Harper

Printed by Halstan & Co Ltd, Amersham, Bucks, UK

ENCHANTED APRIL was originally produced by the Hartford Stage Company (Michael Wilson, Artistic Director) in Hartford, Connecticut, in March 2000. It was directed by Michael Wilson; the set design was by Tony Straiges; the lighting design was by Rui Rita; the original music and sound design were by John Gromada; the costume design was by Jess Goldstein; and the production stage manager was Wendy Beaton. The cast was as follows:

LOTTY WILTON	Isabel Keating
MELLERSH WILTON	John Hines
ROSE ARNOTT	Enid Graham
FREDERICK ARNOTT	Christopher Donahue
CAROLINE BRAMBLE	Stephanie March
ANTONY WILDING	Christopher Duva
MRS GRAVES	Jill Tanner
COSTANZA	Irma St Paule

ENCHANTED APRIL opened on Broadway at the Belasco Theatre on April 29, 2003, produced by Jeffrey Richards/Richard Gross/Ellen Berman, Raymond J and Pearl Berman Greenwald, Irving Welzer, Libby Adler Mages/Mari Glick, Howard R Berlin, Terry E Schnuck and Frederic B Vogel. It was directed by Michael Wilson; the set design was by Tony Straiges; the lighting design was by Rui Rita; the original music and sound design were by John Gromada; the costume design was by Jess Goldstein; and the production stage manager was Katherine Lee Boyer. The cast was as follows:

LOTTY WILTON	Jayne Atkinson
MELLERSH WILTON	Michael Cumpsty
ROSE ARNOTT	Molly Ringwald
FREDERICK ARNOTT	Daniel Gerroll
CAROLINE BRAMBLE	Dagmara Dominczyk
ANTONY WILDING	Michael Hayden
MRS GRAVES	Elizabeth Ashley
COSTANZA	Patricia Conolly

CHARACTERS

LOTTY WILTON, 30, a Hampstead housewife

MELLERSH WILTON, 32, her husband, a solicitor

ROSE ARNOTT, 38, a Hampstead housewife

FREDERICK ARNOTT, 45, her husband, a writer

CAROLINE BRAMBLE, 25, a socialite

ANTONY WILDING, 25, an artist

MRS GRAVES, 70s, a London matron

COSTANZA, 60s, an Italian housekeeper

PLACE

ACT ONE
London, England

ACT TWO
Mezzago, Italy

TIME

1922

ACT ONE

Scene One

Darkness. Half-light rises on two tables, four chairs, a coat rack with coats and umbrellas. ROSE ARNOTT *sits at one table.* LOTTY WILTON *stands at the other, looking off. Thunder, followed by the sound of steady rain. Lights up in a London ladies' club, 1922. "The Great War" is over by four years, and with it the lives of one million British men.* ROSE *reads a copy of the London* Times. LOTTY *gazes out of a large window.*

Both are dressed heavily in dark colours, hair up, with hats on or nearby. LOTTY'S *appearance suggests uncertainty.* ROSE *is spare to the point of severity.* LOTTY *speaks to us. Her essence is of deep sadness and withering valiance, from which genuine hope spontaneously and regularly bursts forth, leaving her endlessly off-balance.*

LOTTY   I was once told the story of a man who, while surveying the grounds of his home, dug his walking stick into the earth, as a reminder of where he wished to one day have an acacia tree. One he could watch from his veranda, and lie under with his wife on warm summer afternoons, cooled in the shadow of its white flowers, and blanketed in their sweet scent. But when planting season came 'round and he returned with a spade and an acacia sapling, the man was vexed. The stick he had left had taken root and begun to grow. It was nearly as tall as himself now, in fact, with young, awkward branches and small clusters of frail new leaves. This, on the very spot that was to be his acacia. The man buried his spade into the ground to unearth the strange thing . . . but stopped. For among the leaves, underneath, he spied a small blossom. (*Enchanted.*) It was acacia. (*Smiles.*) "Enchantment," some would say. Or "providence," perhaps. I suppose the only real certainty is that the fellow had lost a perfectly good walking stick. If that's the part

you choose to see. The rest is open to opinion.
(*Sighs, thinks.*) Were it only that some
enchantment would step in for us all, to change
what we have into what we wish for. To bridge
the awkward gap between all of our many
befores and afters. Because, for every after
found, a before must be lost. And loss is, by
nature, an unbalancing thing. More
unbalancing, however, is to discover your
before gone without an after having taken its
place. Leaving you merely to wait and to
wonder if there is to be an after at all. Or if,
perhaps, waiting and wondering are your after
in themselves. (*Thinks.*) I wasn't expecting my
after to begin that day at my ladies' club. I
wasn't waiting for enchantment to show itself,
or providence. I had merely been gazing out of
the window, wondering if the rain was ever
going to stop. And what my husband might like
for dinner that night. And about the fact that
the day before I had wondered the same things.
And surely would the following day, and the
day after that, and the day after. When I came
upon the advertisement.

ROSE   (*reading*) "To those who appreciate wisteria
            and sunshine . . . "

LOTTY   A small advert, placed discreetly in the agony
            column of the *Times*.

ROSE   "Small castle on the Mediterranean, Northern
            Italy . . ."

LOTTY   Heaven!

ROSE   "To be let for the month of April. Cook,
            gardens, ocean view. Reply Box Eleven."

LOTTY   (*beaming*) The words washed over me, filling
            me suddenly with warmth and peacefulness, as
            if the advertisement were there especially for
            me, and was pleased I'd found it. "To those
            who appreciate wisteria and sunshine." That's

me! (*Thunder. Thinks.*) But who am I to be reading about Italian castles, and Aprils on the Mediterranean? Who am I? (*Inspired.*) But then, why would I bother to read the newspaper at my ladies' club, when I surely would read my husband's copy tomorrow morning after housekeeping? And why would I come to my club at all on a Tuesday, when my regular city day is Wednesday? And certainly why would I notice the lady, that particular lady I see so often at church, and was thinking of only moments ago? Providence? Enchantment? (*She smiles excitedly. To* ROSE, *with great enthusiasm.*) Are you reading about the castle and the wisteria?

ROSE   (*invaded, stone-faced throughout*) I beg your pardon?

LOTTY   (*breathlessly*) The advertisement about the castle. It sounds so wonderful, doesn't it? Can you just imagine? Italy and sunshine and wisteria. And when I saw you . . . you, of all people . . . well, I couldn't help but think . . . well, I mean, all this rain . . . and, oh, the Mediterranean . . . imagine . . . and this not even being my city day . . . well, I . . . I . . . (*Flustered, suddenly painfully uncomfortable, realizing that her intensity has once again escaped.*) Oh, I am sorry. Here we've only just met and I must apologize already. My husband says that my mind is like a hummingbird. One seldom sees it land. I feel I know you. And yet we've never actually met. My husband and I see you in church in Hampstead.

ROSE   I see.

LOTTY   You are our "disappointed Madonna." I see you each Sunday, marshalling in the children from Sunday School, always so right on time for services, and with the schoolchildren so very well-behaved. And I once commented to my husband that you looked to me somewhat like a disappointed Madonna.

ROSE   (*looking about self-consciously*) I . . .

LOTTY   My husband had been speaking to me about finding satisfaction through doing one's job well. Saying something about that if one does one's job well, then one will *not* be depressed, but will instead be automatically bright and brisk with satisfaction. And, seeing you, I just felt that . . . well, that surely there is also the chance for a certain . . . disappointment.

ROSE   (*patiently*) Perhaps it would be best if we begin at the beginning. I am Mrs Arnott. Rose.

LOTTY   Thank you. I am Lotty. Charlotte. Mrs Wilton.

ROSE   Right, then.

LOTTY   (*sadly*) I don't expect that conveys much to you, "Wilton." Sometimes it doesn't seem to convey anything to me, either. Such a small, sad name. I don't like names.

ROSE   Do you need some kind of advice, Mrs Wilton?

LOTTY   Oh, no. It was just the advertisement. It sounded so wonderful, that's all.

ROSE   I'm sure it's only this gloomy weather that makes it seem so.

LOTTY   Then you were reading it?

ROSE   (*caught*) I . . . was.

LOTTY   (*excitedly*) I knew it! I saw it!

ROSE   Saw it?

LOTTY   The two of us. At the castle.

ROSE   Yourself and your husband.

LOTTY   Oh no, me and you!

ROSE   (*losing her patience, self-consciously hushed*)
                Mrs Wilton!

LOTTY   Do you ever see things in a kind of a flash
                before they happen?

ROSE   Never.

LOTTY   Really? Well, when I saw you, I suddenly saw
                us both, you and me, on the shores of the
                Mediterranean. Surrounded by beauty. Beauty
                and blissful peace.

ROSE   Really, Mrs Wilton. And our husbands?

                (LOTTY *thinks.*)

LOTTY   I didn't see them. I've never seen Mr Arnott.
                He is "with us," then?

ROSE   Oh, yes. Quite.

LOTTY   One never knows these days. So many war
                widows.

ROSE   (*sincerely*) Sad times.

LOTTY   Perhaps that's why we need something
                beautiful now. To remind us of the possibility. I
                did see us, Rose.

ROSE   Well, that is really most extraordinary, Mrs
                Wilton.

LOTTY   Isn't it? Isn't it wonderful enough just to think
                about? April in Italy. And here it's February
                already. In two months we could be in it all.

ROSE   It's easy to think of such things, Mrs Wilton.
          But it's no use wasting one's time thinking too
          long.

LOTTY   Oh, but it is! It's essential! And I really do
          believe, if one considers hard enough, things
          can happen!

ROSE   I'm not sure I believe that.

LOTTY   (*becoming increasingly emotional*) But you
          must! Even if it isn't true. I've been saving a
          nest egg, from my dress allowance. It's not
          much, but my husband himself encouraged me
          to save it for a rainy day. My husband speaks
          often of rainy days. My husband speaks often
          of many things. I could never have imagined
          spending it on a holiday, but if this isn't that
          rainy day, well . . .

ROSE   Money, I fear . . .

LOTTY   Rose. Close your eyes and think with all of
          your heart of getting away from Hampstead,
          from husbands, from this relentless rain, from
          everything. To heaven!

ROSE   You shouldn't say things like that, Mrs Wilton.

LOTTY   But it would be heavenly!

ROSE   Heaven isn't somewhere else. It is here and
          now, within us. We are told that on the very
          highest authority. The kindred points of
          heaven and home. Heaven is in our home.

          (LOTTY *thinks.*)

LOTTY   But it isn't.

ROSE   But it is. It is there, if we choose, if we make it.

LOTTY   (*upset, near tears*) I do choose, and I do make
          it. And it isn't. I've done nothing but what was

expected of me all of my life, and thought that was goodness. I thought I would be . . . well . . . rewarded in some way, I suppose. That's selfish, I know. But it was what I was told. One prepares, is good, and is rewarded. I didn't know how quickly things change. That one must keep an eye on what one is preparing for, in case it no longer even exists. Someone forgot to tell me that. Where everyone is racing to, I don't know. I only know that I've been left behind. No. Now I'm convinced that there are blind sorts of goodness and there are . . . enlightened sorts of goodness. Women such as ourselves have been living the blind sort. Preparing for nothing but . . . oblivion.

ROSE   (*flummoxed, scowling*) Mrs Wilton. I assure you that I am a most happy individual.

LOTTY   (*defeated*) Yes. Of course. Will you believe that I have never in my life spoken like this to anyone?

ROSE   It's the weather, I'm sure.

LOTTY   (*lost*) Yes. And the advertisement.

ROSE   Yes.

LOTTY   And both of us being so miserable. (*Sadly.*) Something has been lost, Rose. Something has shifted, and I don't recognize anything anymore.

ROSE   (*moved*) We must all deal with loss, Mrs Wilton. Each in his way.

LOTTY   Yes. That's true. But don't you ever wish you could go back, to hold on tighter? But we can't, can we? We can only go forward. But how? This I haven't seen.

ROSE   Do you see things often, Mrs Wilton?

LOTTY   Lotty. Yes, I do. But seeing and doing are two
                 different things, aren't they? (*They think.*) "To
                 those who appreciate wisteria and sunshine."
                 (LOTTY *smiles wistfully.*) That's you and me,
                 Rose. That much I do see.

                 (*Thunder. Half-light.*)

                 Scene Two

*Rain. Lights up in the Wilton home. A table, two chairs, a
coat rack with coats and umbrellas.* MELLERSH WILTON *sits at
the table, looking into a small table mirror, trimming his
moustache. A towel is draped around his neck,
underneath which he is dressed for an evening business
engagement, save for an untied tie.* LOTTY *prepares herself
hurriedly around him.*

MELLERSH   (*who believes his image to be of premature
                 wisdom, a misconception redeemed somewhat
                 by a deeper vein of abject terror – he speaks
                 to* LOTTY *without looking at her*) Charlotte! It's
                 unlike you to be late and make us have to hurry
                 so. A wife's impunctuality always reflects
                 poorly on the husband, I believe, if not in one
                 way, then in another.

LOTTY   I'm sorry, Mellersh.

MELLERSH   At the least it conveys a lack of concern on her
                 part, and, at the most, a lack of control on his.

LOTTY   Forgive me, Mellersh, but I got into a most
                 interesting conversation at my ladies' club.

MELLERSH   That's all very well, but . . .

LOTTY   Do you know a gentleman from here in
                 Hampstead by the name of Arnott?

MELLERSH   Why? What has he done?

LOTTY	Oh, nothing that I'm aware of. I'm sure he's quite the usual, in fact. I just thought you might know him through business.
MELLERSH	The name's not familiar. It will look very bad if we are late, Charlotte.
LOTTY	I am sorry, Mellersh. I wish that you would just go without me, really. You know I only feel awash with these artistic sorts.
MELLERSH	But a family solicitor must show his family, now, mustn't he? It's not so important that you enjoy yourself, but that you simply are there. (*He checks his teeth.*)
LOTTY	It's just that I always feel so . . . negligible. I never know what to say. And if, by chance, I do have something to say, it only comes out wrong.
MELLERSH	If you're asked for your opinion, you need merely say "marvelous," or something of that nature, and leave it at that. That's all they want to hear anyhow. Try it.
LOTTY	"Marvelous."
MELLERSH	You'll be surprised how far it will get you.
LOTTY	It's Impressionists again, then?
MELLERSH	Why?
LOTTY	It's all just a bit of a muddle. To my eye.
MELLERSH	Sometimes one has to step back a bit. Have you tried that?
LOTTY	And then what?
MELLERSH	And then . . . "Marvelous." It's not so much the artists I'm interested in, anyhow, but their

	patrons and sponsors, who might be in need of legal counsel.
LOTTY	I understand. Might we go to dinner afterward?
MELLERSH	We will eat at home. Where have you put my *Times*, Charlotte?
LOTTY	"Times," Mellersh?
MELLERSH	Yes.
LOTTY	You mean the newspaper?
MELLERSH	Of course the . . . have you taken leave of your senses? What else would I mean by "my *Times*"?
LOTTY	(*busying herself nervously*) Of course that's what you meant. (MELLERSH *waits.*)
MELLERSH	Well?
LOTTY	Well what, Mellersh?
MELLERSH	(*steadying himself*) Where have you put today's *Times*?
LOTTY	It seems I forgot to pick one up. (MELLERSH *eyes her,* LOTTY *moves on.*)
MELLERSH	I shall miss it now.
LOTTY	Yes. Perhaps it would be best if, in future, you picked up your own *Times*.
MELLERSH	But you pick up my *Times,* Charlotte. I see no reason to change procedure now. You need merely be sure to remember.
LOTTY	Yes, but . . .
MELLERSH	(*raising a hand*) Case closed, my dear. Case closed. (LOTTY *burns.*)

LOTTY   Mellersh?

MELLERSH   Yes?

LOTTY   Do you know what the weather is like in Italy in April?

MELLERSH   Quite lovely, I imagine. Why do you ask?

LOTTY   Oh, no reason, really. We were just talking about it today. About holidays.

MELLERSH   And what were you discussing about holidays?

LOTTY   Just that they must be nice, that's all.

MELLERSH   I'm certain they are. Although I have heard some shocking stories to the contrary. There is an inherent element of risk in holidays that tends to color quite nicely the sureties of home.

             (LOTTY *thinks*.)

LOTTY   The piano needs tuning.

MELLERSH   What made you think of that?

LOTTY   I don't know. It doesn't matter. Unless, of course, you think I should tune it myself.

MELLERSH   Charlotte.

LOTTY   I'm ready, Mellersh. (MELLERSH *looks up. LOTTY is glowing with thrift*.)

MELLERSH   Right, then.

LOTTY   Do I look all right, Mellersh?

MELLERSH   Fine, fine. You do manage quite well with your dress allowance, my dear. Your ability with thrift is highly admirable.

LOTTY   The sureties of home.

MELLERSH   And much appreciated for it. (*He kisses two fingers and touches her nose.*)

LOTTY   Off we go, then. (*Starts to exit.*)

MELLERSH   (*taken aback*) Charlotte?!

LOTTY   Yes, Mellersh? (*He stares expectantly. She waits, suddenly realizes.*) How silly of me. (*She goes to him, ties his tie.* MELLERSH *thinks, quite used to being attended to.*)

MELLERSH   Do you think this Arnott is someone I should look up?

LOTTY   Oh, no. I didn't mean that. I don't know anything about him, really. I only met his wife, that's all.

MELLERSH   Well, that's very clever of you. You can make many connections for me at your ladies' club, I imagine, if you steer your conversation in a useful direction.

LOTTY   Yes, Mellersh, I'm sure.

            (MELLERSH *thinks.*)

MELLERSH   I will miss my *Times,* Charlotte.

LOTTY   I am sorry. There shall be another tomorrow. (MELLERSH *sighs with great patience. The tie is tied.*) There.

MELLERSH   Right, then. Now . . . (*Takes a monocle from his pocket, places it, poses.*) How do I look?

            (LOTTY *looks him over.*)

LOTTY   Marvelous.

            (*Thunder. Half-light.*)

Scene Three

Rain. Lights up in the Arnott home. A table, two chairs, a coat rack with coats and umbrellas. FREDERICK ARNOTT *stands at his mirror, tying his tie, preparing himself for a social engagement. He is jovial and in a party mood, singing "Ma, He's Making Eyes At Me" to himself between poses.* ROSE *enters, returning from the club.*

ROSE   (*surprised*) Frederick.

FREDERICK   Rose.

ROSE   You're here.

FREDERICK   Here I am.

ROSE   And there you go, it seems. Who is it tonight?

FREDERICK   The Bacon-Cateses. A party for my new book.

ROSE   (*coldly*) That should be a posh set.

FREDERICK   Hurry and you can join me.

ROSE   Wouldn't that be comical.

                (FREDERICK *picks up a book and pen.*)

FREDERICK   *Madame DuBarry* has all the appearance of being my most successful book yet, even more so than *Pompadour*. The Bacon-Cateses never invited me for *Madame Pompadour*. (*He opens the book and signs.*) Sin must have taken a step up in respectability if even the Bacon-Cateses have asked for the pleasure of meeting "Mr Florian Ayers."

ROSE   Sin cannot take a step up, Frederick. And you know how I feel about that name.

FREDERICK   (*rolling the name off of his tongue*) "Florian
             Ayers." Even you must admit that as a pen
             name, it is most imaginative.

ROSE   Your imagination has never been in question.

FREDERICK   Yes. Well, don't dislike that name too much,
             darling. When God comes to browse through
             my literary *oeuvre,* He'll damn "Florian Ayers"
             straight to Hell, but you and I shall be spared.
             (*He smiles.* ROSE *does not respond.*) There was
             a time when you laughed at my humor, Rose.
             You could light up a room when you laughed.

ROSE   That was before.

FREDERICK   Before my books, you mean? My poetry never
             afforded charity. Your church should be
             thanking Madame DuBarry. Those boots you
             bought the schoolchildren this winter? Stout
             with sin.

ROSE   I didn't mean your books. (*She thinks.*) You
             were a good poet, Frederick. And Frederick
             Arnott is a good name.

FREDERICK   To whom?

ROSE   To me.

FREDERICK   Rose. I am a weak and wicked man. I wish you
             could forgive me that.

ROSE   You are not wicked, Frederick.

FREDERICK   You're right. "Florian Ayers" is wicked. I'm
             merely weak.

ROSE   It's just . . . one should not write books God
             would not like to read. (FREDERICK *laughs.*)

FREDERICK   Madame DuBarry has nothing over Mary
             Magdalene, I assure you.

ROSE   Is everything funny to you?

FREDERICK   No darling, it's not. God knows.

ROSE   Does He? We are judged by our actions,
                        Frederick, not by our intentions.

FREDERICK   He's keeping score you say?

ROSE   Something like that.

FREDERICK   And what of those who say we are loved all the
                        more for our . . . humanness?

                        (ROSE *thinks*.)

ROSE   I would say that they are mistaken. (*Moving
                        toward him*.) Here. You've muffed your tie.

FREDERICK   (*pulling away*) I have it.

ROSE   Do you know anyone by the name of Wilton?

FREDERICK   Wilton?

ROSE   A solicitor and his wife. (FREDERICK *shudders*.)

FREDERICK   I make quite a point of avoiding solicitors.

ROSE   I met the wife today. A most unusual woman.

FREDERICK   (*enthused*) Really?

ROSE   She spoke of heaven and home.

FREDERICK   (*disappointed*) Oh. (*He starts to sing*.)

ROSE   And of loss. She claims to see things. She said
                        that I looked to her like a disappointed
                        Madonna. What is that exactly?

FREDERICK   What is what?

ROSE   The song you're singing.

FREDERICK   Just a little jazz number I've heard. (*Sings to*
                 ROSE, *dancing.*) "Ma, he's making eyes at me!
                 Ma, he's awful nice to me!"

ROSE   "Making eyes"?

FREDERICK   Yes. You know . . . (*He gives her a seductive
                 look.*) Valentino. (ROSE *finds the image a bit
                 more appealing than she'd like.*)

ROSE   Chaplin, perhaps. (*She pulls away, thinks.*)
                 This Mrs Wilton. She wondered how one is to
                 go forward when so much has been lost.

FREDERICK   (*concerned*) Exactly what did the two of you
                 discuss?

ROSE   Nothing specific. I'm not at all certain she
                 heard a word I said, actually.

FREDERICK   Rose. My book tour lasts from the end of
                 March through all of April. Come with me.

ROSE   (*looking at him, moved*) April? With you?
                 (*Thinks.*) As what? "Mrs Florian Ayers"?
                 Really, you and Mrs Wilton are two of a kind.
                 (*Hands him the book.*) You don't want to miss
                 your party.

FREDERICK   No. (*He gets his hat, starts to exit, defeated.*)
                 Rose? Should the things you have faith in ever
                 include the people who love you . . . (*He pops
                 his hat on his head.*) . . . be in touch.

                 (*Thunder. Half-light.*)

                            Scene Four

Rain. Lights up in a church. ROSE *is searching for something.*
LOTTY *enters, glancing over her shoulder.*

LOTTY   (*whispering loudly*) Mrs Arnott! Rose!

ROSE   (*aghast*) Mrs Wilton!

LOTTY   I've only a moment. I told Mellersh I left my
            gloves in our pew.

ROSE   Lying to your husband, Mrs Wilton, in Our
            Father's house?

LOTTY   Oh, but I didn't lie. I really left them, so that I
            wouldn't be lying. (*She retrieves her gloves.*
            ROSE *looks heavenward, sighs.*) I got it, Rose!
            A reply to our inquiry about the castle!

ROSE   (*sternly*) Please. We really must talk.

LOTTY   It is most kind, from a Mr Antony Wilding, of
            Knightsbridge. It smells of cinnamon!

ROSE   Cinnamon?

LOTTY   Isn't that delightful! But, brace yourself. Sixty
            pounds for the month of April.

ROSE   Mrs Wilton . . .

LOTTY   I know it would be a stretch for us both.

ROSE   Corresponding with someone we know nothing
            of. We've gone too far already.

LOTTY   Rose.

ROSE   And all of this talk of money. Please. It has,
            indeed, been grand dreaming of this. But no
            further.

LOTTY   But, Rose.

ROSE   (*taking a stand*) I have made up my mind, Mrs
            Wilton.

LOTTY   Lotty. If it's only the money, then I have an
            idea.

ROSE	It is not only the money.
LOTTY	I thought perhaps if we advertise for traveling companions . . .
ROSE	Companions?
LOTTY	Ladies. There must be dozens of ladies in our situation who would enjoy sharing such a holiday. Not that we'd want dozens, of course. But another couple, say, would certainly ease the burden.
ROSE	Please . . . we really mustn't discuss this here. It's wrong. I feel as if we're plotting.
LOTTY	But we are! Plotting our escape! Have you lost something?
ROSE	One of the schoolchildren somehow misplaced his boots and stockings during services.

(LOTTY *laughs*.)

LOTTY	"Put thy shoes from off thy feet, for this is holy ground."
ROSE	Angus O'Shea is no Moses. As any number of schoolgirls will tell you.
LOTTY	Rose . . .
ROSE	You've taken leave of your senses, Mrs Wilton.
LOTTY	Don't say that!
ROSE	Start with your nest egg. What if there is an actual need?
LOTTY	This is an actual need.
ROSE	I don't want to hear any more.

LOTTY   But Rose . . . if we don't go forward . . . well . . . (*Inspired.*) . . . we will be depriving two perfectly innocent traveling companions of their holiday. Two good, unhappy ladies like ourselves. Perhaps in even greater need than ourselves.

                      (ROSE *thinks.*)

ROSE   (*strongly*) You are a bully, Mrs Wilton!

LOTTY   Meet me at the club on Wednesday for tea.

ROSE   Yes. No!

LOTTY   We can compose our advert.

ROSE   Mrs Wilton!

LOTTY   Lotty, Rose. You really must call me Lotty.

ROSE   We are not placing an advertisement, because we are not responding to Mr Wilding.

LOTTY   But I have.

ROSE   What?

LOTTY   I have sent him my nest egg, as a deposit.

ROSE   (*stunned*) Lotty.

LOTTY   It is done, Rose. The castle is ours! (*Thunder. They look heavenward.*) Have you told your husband?

ROSE   Of course not.

LOTTY   We should tell them. (*Thinks.*) Even Moses asked permission.

ROSE   (*near tears*) Please stop talking about Moses.

LOTTY   You're right. It's more like David and Goliath.
               Rose. All I'm asking for is your faith.

               (MELLERSH *calls from outside.*)

MELLERSH   (*offstage*) Charlotte!

LOTTY   Gad! It's Goliath. Wednesday! (*She starts to
               exit.*)

ROSE   (*lost*) Husbands, Lotty!

               (LOTTY *stops.*)

LOTTY   What?

ROSE   Husbands.

LOTTY   Yes. Isn't it terrible. But who could resist an
               invitation to heaven? (*Imagining.*) "Two ladies
               seek other ladies who appreciate . . ."

               (*Blend to Scene Five.*)

                          Scene Five

The home of CAROLINE BRAMBLE. *A table, two chairs, a coat
rack with coats and umbrellas.* CAROLINE *enters, reading from
the* Times.

CAROLINE   " . . . seek other ladies who appreciate wisteria
               and sunshine."

               (LOTTY *and* ROSE *sit attentively.* CAROLINE
               *wears a loose, colourful silk negligée. Her
               youthfulness shines through a weary air. She
               prepares a glass of aspirin powder and lights
               a cigarette, clearly hung-over.*)

LOTTY   We were so pleased to receive your reply, Lady
               Bramble. Although we never expected that our
               advertisement would attract someone . . . such
               as yourself.

CAROLINE	Oh?
ROSE	We've read about you often in the newspapers, Lady Bramble. Your life seems so . . . full.
CAROLINE	(*with chilly aloofness*) Yes.
ROSE	You do realize that the castle is very quiet and remote.
CAROLINE	I hope so. Is there a telephone?
LOTTY	No.
CAROLINE	Good.
ROSE	Mrs Wilton was telling me, in fact, Lady Bramble, of something she read about your dancing on tables.
CAROLINE	In Paris.
ROSE	Really.
LOTTY	You must be very tired. (*Explaining herself.*) Whenever I see moderns such as yourself I always see a certain . . . weariness. Modernity being such a shifty beast.
CAROLINE	Yes. Have you received many replies to your advertisement?
ROSE	To our surprise, I'm afraid, only two.
LOTTY	The other is from a Mrs Clayton Graves. Do you know her, Lady Bramble?
CAROLINE	I don't believe so.
LOTTY	You know so many people.
CAROLINE	That's just it, I'm afraid. Mother insists on my knowing everyone, or at least on everyone she

knows knowing me. She fancies herself a
"patroness of the arts," which for her simply
means the chance to give parties. An
opportunistic group, artists. They never miss a
party. Always grabbing and making eyes. Now
she's collecting writers, the sorriest lot yet.
Trying to create what's lacking in their own
lives. Do you know any writers?

LOTTY   No. (*They look to* ROSE, *who looks away.*)

CAROLINE   I'm in great need of an escape right now. From
               all of it.

LOTTY   We are of like minds, then, Lady Bramble. Mrs
               Arnott and myself are escaping too!

ROSE   Lotty.

CAROLINE   Escaping? (*Joking.*) You aren't "wanted
               women," are you?

LOTTY   (*laughing*) Oh, Lady Bramble! We're not
               wanted at all! We're just in need of a holiday,
               that's all. And I believe the castle will be the
               perfect place.

CAROLINE   Yes. It seemed so to me as well. I had replied to
               the original advertisement, actually, but was
               answered that someone had already placed a
               deposit.

LOTTY   I do hope we haven't spoiled your plans, Lady
               Bramble.

CAROLINE   Oh, I really didn't care. A month alone had
               seemed appealing. But strange surroundings
               and simple company may prove most
               acceptable.

ROSE   (*smoothly*) We may pale in comparison with
               your usual acquaintances, Lady Bramble, but I
               assure you that Mrs Wilton and myself are by
               no means "simple."

CAROLINE   (*unusually uncertain*) Oh, I never meant that
                you were. What I meant was . . .

LOTTY   No grabbing!

CAROLINE   (*relieved*) Precisely. What I really meant, I
                suppose, is that you aren't . . . men.

LOTTY   (*smiling*) Yes.

ROSE   (*not smiling*) That is true.

CAROLINE   With men it would be impossible to be as . . .
                unrestricted as I'd like. (*She stretches,
                revealing a silky chemise.*)

ROSE   Unrestricted?

CAROLINE   Part of what intrigued me about your
                advertisement is that it would be quite a
                novelty, really, to be among lady friends. I
                haven't many.

LOTTY   Oh?

ROSE   And why do you think that is, Lady Bramble?

CAROLINE   Perhaps at the end of April you could tell me.
                Should I join you. (*Thunder.*) Isn't this rain a
                nuisance?

LOTTY   (*feeling a kinship*) Oh, yes!

CAROLINE   May I offer you a cognac?

ROSE   It is eleven in the morning, Lady Bramble.

CAROLINE   Yes. (*With a hint of sadness.*) May I ask you
                something?

LOTTY   Of course, Lady Bramble.

CAROLINE   Were your husbands lost?

ROSE	Lost?
CAROLINE	In the war.
LOTTY	Well, no, Lady Bramble.
ROSE	Our husbands have not been lost at all, Lady Bramble.
CAROLINE	(*relieved*) Oh. Isn't that funny? You look like widows! Had I seen you on a street corner, I would have been inclined to give you a donation.
ROSE	(*beginning to burn*) Lady Bramble . . .
CAROLINE	I should like to join you at the castle, then.
LOTTY	Grand!
	(ROSE *scowls.*)
CAROLINE	(*aware of* ROSE) And, should we find that things don't work out, I shall simply move on and you may keep my payment in full.
ROSE	But that would be unfair to you, Lady Bramble.
LOTTY	But things will work out, Lady Bramble. You'll see. I'm quite sure we're all going to be the very best of friends. Better than friends! Sisters!
CAROLINE	(*warily*) Yes. Well, let's start then by not calling me Lady Bramble. Mother is Lady Bramble. Call me Lady Caroline.
LOTTY	(*beaming*) Lady Caroline!
CAROLINE	Well. (*She lifts her hand in a graceful salute.*) All'Italia! (LOTTY *and* ROSE *stare, perplexed.* CAROLINE *explains.*) To Italy.

(LOTTY *smiles and lifts her hand, fumbling enthusiastically.*)

LOTTY   All'Italia!

(*They look at* ROSE. *She frowns, considers, lifts her fist with stiff reluctance. Thunder. Half-light.*)

Scene Six

Rain. Lights up in the home of MRS GRAVES. *A table, two chairs, a coat rack with coats and umbrellas.* LOTTY *and* ROSE *are seated, silent.* MRS GRAVES *paces regally. She is heavily dressed, highly proper, and walks with the aid of a stick.*

MRS GRAVES   If we are to spend the whole of a month together, I consider it preferable that certain ground rules be spelled out sooner rather than later. I do not approve of modern language, behaviour or thinking. I find informal idioms of speech unacceptable, and will not tolerate them. I take breakfast promptly at seven in the morning, luncheon at noon, tea at half past four, and dinner at quarter to eight. I like nuts. I am not interested in idle conversation. My only desire is to sit quietly and remember.

ROSE   Yes, well . . .

MRS GRAVES   (*not listening, sitting down to a bowl of nuts*) Although I have great fondness for the Italian seaside, I have no fondness whatsoever for those native customs so many find charming. I would expect such behavior to remain outside of our retreat.

LOTTY   Yes, I'm sure . . .

MRS GRAVES   Now to which of you does the castle belong?

LOTTY   Oh, to none of us, Mrs Graves. We haven't
               even seen it. It was advertised. Mrs Arnott and
               I have rented it.

MRS GRAVES   Rented?! How do you know it isn't a
               dilapidation?

ROSE   We've corresponded with the owner, a Mr
               Antony Wilding. It appears to be most
               agreeable.

LOTTY   There's a private beach, and olive groves, and
               bushels and bushels of wisteria.

               (MRS GRAVES *thinks.*)

MRS GRAVES   I am very fond of wisteria. The house at Box
               Hill was covered with it. I remember once my
               father and I . . .

LOTTY   Your father lived at Box Hill, Mrs Graves?

MRS GRAVES   Of course not. George Meredith lived at Box
               Hill. The writer. My father often took me there
               on invitation.

ROSE   You knew George Meredith, Mrs Graves?

MRS GRAVES   My father traveled among all the great men.
               (*She waves her stick, pointing at
               photographs.*) Carlyle. Arnold. Tennyson.

LOTTY   Tennyson, Rose. Imagine!

MRS GRAVES   As I was saying . . .

LOTTY   (*pointing*) Is that a photograph of Tennyson,
               Mrs Graves?

MRS GRAVES   No. That is a photograph of Mr Clayton
               Graves, my late husband. A sizable difference, I
               assure you. (*She points her stick, barely
               missing* LOTTY *and* ROSE.) *That* is Tennyson.
               And I am the young girl with the pigtail.

Which, I might add, gave the great one no small delight. He would often tell my father . . .

LOTTY (*excitedly*) Did you know Keats, Mrs Graves?

ROSE Lotty! (MRS GRAVES *freezes.*)

MRS GRAVES Keats?!

LOTTY Yes. John Keats. The poet.

MRS GRAVES I am well aware . . . (*Frigidly.*) I did not know Keats, Mrs Wilton.

LOTTY Oh.

MRS GRAVES And if that is the direction in which you are heading, I regret to inform you that I was also unacquainted with Shakespeare.

LOTTY Of course. The immortals seem so alive, don't they? One forgets sometimes that they are dead.

MRS GRAVES Many for quite some time.

LOTTY It was just that I thought I saw Keats the other day.

ROSE Lotty!

MRS GRAVES Saw Keats?!

LOTTY Yes. Crossing the street in Hampstead, in front of his house.

ROSE Mrs Graves . . .

LOTTY But then I suppose it was his ghost, naturally.

(MRS GRAVES *eyes* LOTTY, *who looks at* ROSE, *who looks away, pained.*)

MRS GRAVES Do you have references?

ROSE   Shouldn't we be the ones asking for references
                from you, Mrs Graves?

MRS GRAVES   (*surprised that this came from* ROSE, *gathering
                all of her dignity*) If you must, you may
                communicate with the President of the Royal
                Academy, the Archbishop of Canterbury, and
                the Governor of the Bank of England.

ROSE   I see.

LOTTY   (*deflecting*) Is the large portrait of your father,
                Mrs Graves?

MRS GRAVES   Yes. That is himself. But we were speaking of
                references, Mrs Wilton.

LOTTY   And the other portrait is your mother?

MRS GRAVES   My mother?! That, Mrs Wilton, is the good
                Queen Victoria.

LOTTY   I don't think references are nice things
                between decent English women. We needn't
                distrust each other. We're not Americans.

ROSE   (*rising*) References bring an atmosphere into
                our holiday plan that isn't quite what we want,
                Mrs Graves. Good day. (*She pushes* LOTTY
                toward the exit.)

MRS GRAVES   How are the expenses to be divided?

LOTTY   (*excitedly*) Fifteen pounds each for rent, plus
                food. A real bargain!

MRS GRAVES   I'm an old woman. I don't eat much.

ROSE   That would certainly be your choice to make,
                Mrs Graves.

LOTTY   Perhaps we can catch our own, Mrs Graves.
                How are you with a bow? (MRS GRAVES *is
                stricken again.*)

MRS GRAVES	Your advertisement clearly stated that there would be a cook. My stick prohibits me from entering kitchens.
ROSE	There is a woman by the name of Costanza.
MRS GRAVES	Costan . . . ? Fifteen pounds. Really, ten seems most reasonable, considering the circumstances.
ROSE	Fifteen, Mrs Graves.
LOTTY	Fifteen is fair, Mrs Graves.
MRS GRAVES	The wisteria is guaranteed?
ROSE	Look . . .
LOTTY	Mrs Graves, Mr Wilding has assured us that we shall have wisteria.
MRS GRAVES	(*with great reluctance*) I shall waive references. But no wisteria and I'll expect a deduction.
ROSE	Thank you, Mrs Graves. You've been most . . . (MRS GRAVES *gestures for them to sit. They do.*) I can't seem to find the word I'm looking for.
MRS GRAVES	Is the fourth of our party a widow as well?
	(LOTTY *and* ROSE *look at each other, perplexed.*)
LOTTY	A widow, Mrs Graves? Well, no. Actually . . .
	(MRS GRAVES *raises her hand for silence.*)
MRS GRAVES	(*gravely*) All in good time. All in good time. (*Reciting, frighteningly.*) "Old sisters of a day gone by / Gray nurses, loving nothing new / Why should they miss their yearly due / Before their time? They too will die." (LOTTY *and* ROSE

sit, frozen. MRS GRAVES *cracks a nut, smiles.*)
May I offer you a nut?

(*Thunder. Half-light.*)

Scene Seven

Rain. Lights up in the flat of ANTONY WILDING. *A table, two chairs, a coat rack with coats and umbrellas.* LOTTY *and* ROSE *stand attentively.*

WILDING	Oh yes, the wisteria is everywhere, as advertised. You can see some of the view in these photographs here. (*The ladies turn their eyes away from* WILDING *himself, who wears a loose, open shirt and an even more open smile.*) I took these myself, I'm afraid. You'd hardly mistake them for professionals. (*He turns the photo. They huddle together, turning their heads, squinting.*) It's a small castle, but of course it has most of the "modern improvements," as an estate agent would say. Its name is San Salvatore. *[Salvator-ay.]*
LOTTY/ROSE	(*trying it out*) San Salvatore.
LOTTY	It sounds sacred, Rose.
ROSE	What is that there, Mr Wilding?
WILDING	(*looking at* ROSE, *distracted by something in her face*) What, Mrs Arnott?
ROSE	(*pointing*) That. (*He continues to stare, pulls himself away to look at the photo.*)
WILDING	That, I'm afraid, appears to have been my left thumb. (*The ladies smile discreetly.*) But had it not been there, it would be a view of the sea and of the lower garden. The castle has both upper and lower gardens, with a lovely terrace between. (*He hands them a card.*) For you. A postcard of the village below.

LOTTY/ROSE   (*reading*) Mez-zago.

WILDING   (*to* ROSE, *enunciating*) Met-zago.

ROSE   (*self-consciously*) Met-zago. (WILDING *smiles.*)

WILDING   I like your face, Mrs Arnott. (ROSE *freezes.*) But
              here, let's make you comfortable. (*He removes
              their coats.*) In April, you know, the area is
              simply a mass of flowers. (*Admiring* ROSE'S
              figure. To her.) You must wear white.

ROSE   (*embarrassed*) White?

WILDING   Yes. There's a dock and small boat, if . . . well,
              if your husbands are so inclined.

LOTTY   Our husbands, Mr Wilding? (*In mock
              mourning.*) They will not be with us, I'm afraid.

WILDING   Forgive me. So many widows these days.

ROSE   No . . .

LOTTY   There will be four of us, however. Lady friends.

WILDING   Really? San Salvatore should be filled with
              friends. It can be a bit lonely.

ROSE   Is San Salvatore a family home?

WILDING   Yes. Or it was. I've no longer any family, so it's
              no longer a home, I suppose.

LOTTY   Oh.

WILDING   Father's parents had the place built. A love
              nest of sorts, from the way he told it. I never
              knew them, unfortunately, but some of the
              stories are delightful.

LOTTY   It sounds wonderful.

WILDING   (*at* ROSE) Yes. It's beautiful. (*Pulling away.*) Father loved the place. Mother never cared for it much, really, until her later years alone. And then, while I was away in the Army, she and San Salvatore seemed to become one.

LOTTY   Where did you serve, Mr Wilding? (*His smile fades.*)

WILDING   Flanders, mostly.

LOTTY   (*sincerely*) Brave battles.

ROSE   We are indebted to you, Mr Wilding. (WILDING *nods.*)

WILDING   I lost Mother last year, sad to say. She always said that there was something enchanted about the castle in April. I hate to miss it this year, but I've work in Rome.

ROSE   What is your work, Mr Wilding?

WILDING   I paint. Portraits. Classical, of course. Two eyes, one mouth, and so on.

      (LOTTY *thinks.*)

LOTTY   Marvelous!

WILDING   I've a studio in Bloomsbury. Perhaps you both could visit sometime and be studied. I'm said to have a particular talent with the female form.

      (ROSE *lets out a small gasp.* LOTTY *hurriedly hands an envelope to* WILDING.)

LOTTY   Our final payment, Mr Wilding.

WILDING   Well. (*Takes the envelope.*) Now I'm richer . . . (*He hugs* LOTTY, *to her delight.*) . . . and you're happier. (*He starts toward* ROSE, *but she cringes.*) What would you say to celebrating our union, as it were, over a cup of hot tea?

LOTTY   Oh, that would be lovely.

ROSE   That's very kind, Mr Wilding.

WILDING   Good. Now, I have plain English black, or, for
             the more daring, a Moroccan blend I'm fond of
             with just a dash of cinnamon that goes by the
             rather audacious name of "Indiscreet."

LOTTY   (*bursting out in giggles*) Oh, my! The
             "Indiscreet" sounds most intriguing.

WILDING   Wonderful! And for you, Mrs Arnott? (ROSE
             considers.)

ROSE   I shall have the black.

WILDING   Right. (*Serving.*) Now you must tell me all
             about the friends you are taking.

ROSE   We hardly know a thing about them, really.

LOTTY   We took your lead, Mr Wilding, and placed an
             advertisement.

WILDING   Oh?

LOTTY   There's Lady Caroline Bramble, who likes
             cognac and dancing. And Mrs Clayton Graves,
             who knew Tennyson and likes . . . (*Thinks.*)

ROSE   Nuts.

WILDING   How interesting. Well, I'm certain that you will
             all find San Salvatore to your liking. Mrs
             Arnott, this will sound a bit extraordinary, but
             there is a portrait of you there.

ROSE   A portrait of me?

WILDING   Yes. A Madonna. There's one on the stairs
             really exactly like you.

ROSE   (*stunned*) Well . . . (*Thunder.*)

WILDING   San Salvatore will certainly be a nice change
                from this weather.

LOTTY   Yes.

WILDING   You'll find the place has lots of sunshine,
                whatever else it hasn't got.

ROSE   What else hasn't it got, Mr Wilding?

WILDING   Troubles. Worries. The plumbing is a bit
                antique, but Costanza can help you with that.
                And to think you'll be among it all in only two
                days.

LOTTY   We leave tomorrow.

WILDING   You've squared away all of your affairs?

                (LOTTY *and* ROSE *share a guilty glance.*)

ROSE   A couple of things remain.

                (*Thunder. Half-light.*)

Scene Eight

*Rain. Lights up in both the Arnott and Wilton homes. Two
tables, four chairs.* ROSE *sits alone.* MELLERSH *sits, finishing a
dessert, a napkin hanging from his collar.* LOTTY *tends to him.
The scene is of escalating fury.*

MELLERSH   Well, now. I am the fat cat tonight, aren't I? All
                my favorites for dinner.

LOTTY   Was everything to your liking, Mellersh?

MELLERSH   All quite delicious, my dear. One would think
                this was a special evening of some sort. And
                perhaps it is!

(FREDERICK *enters, foggy from an evening party.*)

FREDERICK   Well, now. You're up late!

ROSE   Yes, Frederick. There's something I need to speak to you about.

LOTTY   May I speak to you about something, Mellersh?

MELLERSH   It so happens I have something to speak to you about as well. You tell me yours, and then I'll tell you mine.

FREDERICK   Could it wait until morning? Once again Mr Ayers was a success, and once again Mr Arnott is exhausted.

LOTTY   No. You first, Mellersh.

MELLERSH   Very well.

FREDERICK   Sometimes I think a little less attention would still do the trick, really.

ROSE   And perhaps a little less champagne.

FREDERICK   No. That helps.

MELLERSH   Do you remember last month your asking me about holidays?

LOTTY   Well, yes, Mellersh. It's funny you should mention that.

ROSE   I wonder if I might have some money.

MELLERSH   I believe it will please you to know . . . that I am taking you!

FREDERICK   So that's it.

ROSE   Extra money, I mean.

LOTTY	"Taking me," Mellersh?
MELLERSH	To Italy!
FREDERICK	(*taking out his billfold*) What is it this time? Boots or Bibles?
ROSE	I'm going away, Frederick.
MELLERSH	Did you hear me? I said that I am taking you on holiday!
LOTTY	That is really the most extraordinary coincidence.
FREDERICK	Going away?
MELLERSH	Coincidence?
ROSE	For a rest.
LOTTY	Yes, really most extraordinary. Because I was just about to tell you that I am . . . going.
ROSE	Someplace by the sea.
MELLERSH	Going? Going where?
LOTTY	To Italy.
FREDERICK	Come with me on my book tour.
MELLERSH	Have you taken leave of your senses, Charlotte?
ROSE	That is impossible, Frederick.
MELLERSH	How could you be going to Italy? Ridiculous!
FREDERICK	It is not impossible!
LOTTY	It is not ridiculous!

FREDERICK   Listen to me, Rose.

LOTTY   Listen to me, Mellersh. I've been invited.

ROSE   I've listened enough.

LOTTY   A friend has invited me. With a home there.

ROSE   I've waited enough.

LOTTY   And I am going.

FREDERICK   So have I.

MELLERSH   You have no friends . . . with homes in Italy!

ROSE   So we agree then.

LOTTY   I have, Mellersh. I've mentioned her to you.

MELLERSH   Who?

FREDERICK   Rose?

LOTTY   Rose.

MELLERSH   Rose?

               (LOTTY *and* ROSE *look at each other.*)

ROSE   We can't go back, Frederick.

MELLERSH   Rose who?

ROSE   We can only go forward.

MELLERSH   You've kept secrets, Charlotte!

FREDERICK   But not alone!

MELLERSH   Secrets are like rust!

FREDERICK   It's been two years, Rose!

MELLERSH	And now I am to believe that you are actually asking me . . .
LOTTY	I am not asking you anything, Mellersh. I'm telling you!
ROSE	I *am* alone, Frederick.
FREDERICK	As am I.
MELLERSH	This is ridiculous!
FREDERICK	(*holding out cash*) Take your money then, Mrs Arnott.
LOTTY	This time tomorrow I shall be on a train.
FREDERICK	I shall write up my itinerary . . .
MELLERSH	Tomorrow?
LOTTY	To Italy!
FREDERICK	. . . should you wish to be in contact.
	(*Thunder.*)
LOTTY	Damn this rain!
MELLERSH	Rain?!
FREDERICK	Just know that you were the one who closed the door, Rose.
MELLERSH	If you think you are taking one step out of that door, Mrs Wilton.
ROSE	(*hopelessly*) I'm sorry, Frederick. (*She takes the money, exits.*)
LOTTY	(*sharply*) I'm sorry, Mellersh.
	(*She snatches the napkin from* MELLERSH'S *collar, exits. A train whistles loud and long.*

MELLERSH *and* FREDERICK *look at each other, stunned. Half-light.*)

VOICE OVER   Signore e signori, avere prego tutti i documenti pronti per il controllo. Grazie, e benvenuti in Italia! *[Ladies and gentlemen, please have your papers ready for inspection. Thank you, and welcome to Italy!]*

Scene Nine

The sound of a train in motion. Lights up on a train compartment. ROSE *reads from an Italian phrase book.* LOTTY *sleeps. Travel bags are at their feet, coats and hats at their sides.*

ROSE   (*gravely trying out words from the book*) Smarrito. Mi scusi, mi sono smarrito. No. Mi sono smarri-ta. I am lost, feminine. Mi scusi, mi sono smarrita. *[Excuse me, I am lost.]*

(*Lights flash and the train whistles loudly as it passes through a tunnel.* LOTTY *awakens, frightened.*)

LOTTY   Mellersh!

ROSE   (*nervously*) It was only a tunnel, Lotty. Tunnel. (*She thumbs through the book.*) Tunnel.

LOTTY   (*looking out of the compartment window*) Have we crossed the Italian border?

ROSE   I can't tell. It's so dark out. We're running so late.

LOTTY   I wish we were there.

ROSE   We are in God's hands now, Lotty.

LOTTY   I can't see a thing. Why is the window damp?

ROSE   It's raining.

(LOTTY *nearly loses all hope.*)

LOTTY	I'm sure Italian rain is better than English rain.
ROSE	We were expected hours ago. We'll never find our way alone.
LOTTY	When we get to Genoa, Mr Wilding said we need merely ask for Mez-zago.
ROSE	Met-zago.
LOTTY	Why do they pronounce it "Met-zago"? It doesn't have a "t." (*She takes the book from* ROSE*, looks through it.*)
ROSE	(*adrift*) You're certain you saw us at San Salvatore, Lotty?
LOTTY	Yes, Rose.
ROSE	And Lady Caroline and Mrs Graves? Did you also see them?
LOTTY	No. I didn't.
ROSE	They aren't the ladies I would have chosen.
LOTTY	Perhaps they've been chosen for us. When we get to San Salvatore, let's prepare everything for them, shall we? Make things perfect for their arrival.
ROSE	That would be proper.
LOTTY	We can choose the rooms that would please them, and fill them with flowers.
ROSE	If there *are* flowers.
LOTTY	There will be. There must be.

(*They look out, lost. Train sounds steadily increase.*)

ROSE   What is the Italian for "help"?

LOTTY   Oh, Rose.

ROSE   Please, Lotty. Look it up. (LOTTY *does so.* ROSE *stands, panicking.*) How do we stop the train?

LOTTY   We can't stop the train, Rose.

ROSE   (*dressing*) I'm sure if we simply explain that there has been a dreadful mistake.

LOTTY   This is not a mistake.

ROSE   (*forcefully irate*) I told you that I was a happy individual. And I was. I am. Happy! But you spoke of peace. And . . . and of sisters. And . . . and cinnamon! And you got my head quite turned around. You're not a hummingbird at all, Lotty Wilton. You're a hawk! Clear-eyed and . . . and . . . Why aren't you dressing?!

(LOTTY *holds up the book.*)

LOTTY   "Aiuto."

ROSE   What?

LOTTY   The Italian for "help." "Aiuto."

(ROSE *crumbles, sitting.*)

ROSE   (*adrift*) Aiuto.

(*The ladies fall silent, lost in thought.*)

LOTTY   It isn't fair, Rose. To think that we ought to be so happy now, and we're not. (*Sighs.*) Husbands.

ROSE   (*sighs*) Husbands. (*Train sounds rise.* ROSE
                begins to pray.) Aiuto. Mi sono smarrita.

LOTTY   It's going to be lovely, Rose.

ROSE   Mi scusi!

LOTTY   It's going to be heaven.

ROSE   (*dropping to her knees*) Perdonna me!

LOTTY   Sunshine!

ROSE   Aiuto!

LOTTY   Wisteria!

ROSE   Aiuto!

                (*Another tunnel.* LOTTY *drops to her knees in
                fright, begins praying.*)

LOTTY   Aiuto!

ROSE   What have we done, Lotty? What have we
                done?!

LOTTY   I don't know, Rose. But whatever it is . . . (*She
                looks at* ROSE, *then heavenward.*) . . . we've
                done it!

                (*The train whistles loud and long as darkness
                envelops them. End of Act One.*)

ACT TWO

Scene One

Lights up on the terrace at San Salvatore, the following morning. A table and chairs, a chaise. Exits from the terrace into the villa and into the garden. The impression of beautiful garden surroundings, sunshine. COSTANZA *sits at the table, singing to herself, snapping beans and placing them in a large bowl. She is dressed in simple, comfortable clothing and sandals.* CAROLINE *reclines on the chaise in a thin summer ensemble, reading a book.* MRS GRAVES *enters from the villa, carrying a small pitcher. She walks with her stick and is dressed much too warmly for the weather, from high-buttoned shoes to a rather imposing hat. She holds out the pitcher.*

MRS GRAVES   What is this?!

(CAROLINE *and* COSTANZA *shiver, their patience already waning.*)

COSTANZA   (*looking heavenward*) Santa Maria! (*Sighs, resigned.*) Cosa ho fatto adesso, Signora? Qual è il problema adesso? *[What have I done now, Madame? What problem have you found now?]*

MRS GRAVES   You may rattle on and on all you wish, my friend, and I still will not understand you. I speak only the Italian of Dante.

COSTANZA   Cosa c'è? Qual è l'argomento? *[What is it? What is the matter?]*

MRS GRAVES   Lady Caroline, would you please determine from Costanza the origin of this milk.

(COSTANZA *gets up to look at the contents of the pitcher.*)

CAROLINE   The "origin," Mrs Graves?

MRS GRAVES   Yes. (CONSTANZA *takes the pitcher.*)

CAROLINE   You mean the vendor?

MRS GRAVES   I mean the animal.

                (MRS GRAVES *goes to the table, pulls a large
                bell and playing cards from her pockets,
                staking her claim.*)

COSTANZA   (*to* CAROLINE) Il latte è buono, Donna Carolina.
                [The milk is good.]

CAROLINE   Sì, sì. La Signora vorrebbe sapere che tipo di
                latte è questo, Costanza. *[The lady would like
                to know what kind of milk this is, Costanza.]*

COSTANZA   Che tipo di latte, Signorina? Non capisco. È
                latte! *[What kind of milk, Miss? I don't
                understand. It's milk.]*

CAROLINE   La signora vorrebbe sapere . . . l'animale. *[The
                lady would like to know the animal.]*

COSTANZA   L'animale? *[The animal?]* (*She eyes* MRS
                GRAVES.) Eh! Una mucca, naturalmente, Donna
                Carolina. *[A cow, of course.]*

CAROLINE   Sì, grazie, Costanza. Sono spiacente per il
                problema. *[I'm sorry for the problem.]*

COSTANZA   (*already charmed by* CAROLINE) Il problema
                non e con voi, Signorina. *[The problem is not
                with you, Miss.]* (*She eyes* MRS GRAVES. *Under
                her breath.*) Animale! (*She retrieves the bowl
                and exits into the villa.*)

MRS GRAVES   (*sitting*) What was she saying?

CAROLINE   Nothing of concern. Cow.

MRS GRAVES   What?!

CAROLINE   It is cow's milk. It seems Italian milk also comes from cows. (*She rises to retrieve another pillow, returns to the chaise.*)

MRS GRAVES   You look as if you had nothing on underneath.

CAROLINE   I haven't.

MRS GRAVES   How very imprudent. And how highly improper.

CAROLINE   But there are no men here, so how can it be improper? Have you noticed how difficult it is to be improper without men?

MRS GRAVES   God is a man, Lady Caroline. God is a man.

(LOTTY *rushes from the villa in a white nightgown, barefooted and wide-eyed. She looks out at the gardens and sea, but then she sees* CAROLINE *and* MRS GRAVES.)

LOTTY   Oh!

CAROLINE   Good morning.

LOTTY   Lady Caroline!

MRS GRAVES   (*disapprovingly*) You've arrived.

LOTTY   MRS Graves. Yes, late last night. But . . .

MRS GRAVES   Without clothing, apparently.

(ROSE *rushes in, also in a white nightgown, also barefooted and wide-eyed, clutching her Italian phrase book. She sees* CAROLINE *and* MRS GRAVES *and is embarrassed.*)

ROSE   Oh! Ladies! Excuse me!

LOTTY   Yes, excuse us, Mrs Graves, Lady Caroline. We hadn't thought you'd arrived.

CAROLINE   Here we are!

LOTTY   Yes. Not that we're not happy to see you. It's
                 just a great disappointment.

                 (CAROLINE *and* MRS GRAVES *glance at each
                 other, questioning.*)

ROSE   What Lotty means is that we'd planned to give
                 you such a welcome. We were going to choose
                 the nicest rooms for you.

CAROLINE   We've done that.

ROSE   And we meant to make them pretty for you with
                 flowers.

MRS GRAVES   Costanza has seen to everything. In her way.

CAROLINE   Mrs Graves and I arrived yesterday morning.
                 (*Wincing.*) Together.

LOTTY   (*looking out, entranced*) Look at this place,
                 Rose. When I woke this morning, I prepared
                 myself to accept whatever I found. But I
                 couldn't have imagined. The flowers!
                 Snapdragons and periwinkles! Daphnes and
                 iris! And lavender! And cherry trees! And
                 wisteria, Mrs Graves, simply tumbling over
                 itself!

MRS GRAVES   (*disappointed*) Yes.

LOTTY   And sunshine! (*She raises her face to the sun.*)
                 Heaven! Look up "heaven," Rose. (ROSE *opens
                 the phrase book, does so. A distant church
                 bell rings.* LOTTY *drinks it in.*) Listen! Their
                 church bell sounds so light and inviting! Our
                 church bell never sounded like that.

                 (MRS GRAVES *rings her bell furiously. The
                 ladies jump.*)

MRS GRAVES   (*bellowing*) Costanza!

ROSE   It appears you two have everything under
                  control.

MRS GRAVES   It does save time.

LOTTY   Rose! Remember Mr Wilding said that there
                  was an upstairs sitting room with a view. Let's
                  go first thing after breakfast. I suddenly want
                  to write to everyone I know!

MRS GRAVES   That is *my* sitting room, Mrs Wilton.

LOTTY   *Your* sitting room?

MRS GRAVES   I am an old woman. I need a place to myself.

ROSE   But it is a sitting room, Mrs Graves.

MRS GRAVES   There is another room you and Mrs Wilton may
                  use downstairs at the back next to Costanza's
                  room. I must have quiet. (*She rings the bell.*)
                  Your bedrooms were acceptable?

LOTTY   Oh . . .

ROSE   Cozy.

MRS GRAVES   There were two beds in my room, filling it up
                  unnecessarily, so I had one taken out. It has
                  made it much more agreeable.

LOTTY   That's why I have two beds in my room.

ROSE   I have two in mine as well.

MRS GRAVES   Yours must be Lady Caroline's second bed.
                  She also had hers removed.

LOTTY   I see. What was it, Rose?

ROSE   What?

LOTTY   (*weakly*) "Heaven." (ROSE *returns to the book.*)
                  You are chic, Lady Caroline.

MRS GRAVES   She needs a hat. One mustn't get too much sun too soon, Mrs Wilton.

ROSE   (*finding the word, flatly*) "Paradiso." Heaven.

              (COSTANZA *enters from the villa.*)

COSTANZA   (*seeing* LOTTY *and* ROSE, *pleased*) Ah, buona mattina, Signore! Scusatemi. *[Good morning, ladies! Excuse me.]* (*Stonefaced to* MRS GRAVES.) Si, Signora?*[Yes, Madame?]*

MRS GRAVES   It is time for breakfast.

COSTANZA   Adesso? *[Now?]*

MRS GRAVES   (*shouting*) Breakfast!

COSTANZA   Sì, sì, Signora. "Breakfast." (*Instructing.*) "Colazione." (*To* MRS GRAVES' *back.*) Capitalista!(*She exits.*)

MRS GRAVES   I saw to it breakfast was delayed one hour for your first day. It will not be done again. (*Standing.*) Come, ladies. We must be punctual or Costanza will take it as a sign that she too may be lax.

ROSE   (*taking a stand*) Mrs Graves.

MRS GRAVES   Yes?

ROSE   About the sitting room.

MRS GRAVES   What?

LOTTY   (*smoothly*) We are only too glad for you to have it, if it makes you happy, Mrs Graves. We wouldn't have suggested using it had we known. (MRS GRAVES *tries to understand* LOTTY's *intentions, decides not to bother, begins to exit into the villa.*) Not until you had invited us, anyhow. As I'm sure you soon shall. (MRS GRAVES *stops in disbelief.*)

MRS GRAVES	(*to* LOTTY) Do pull yourself together! (*She exits.* LOTTY *sighs happily.*)
LOTTY	We had so hoped to prepare things before your arrival, Lady Caroline.
CAROLINE	Everything has been seen to.
LOTTY	It must be very assuring to be independent, and to know exactly what one wants.
CAROLINE	Quite.
ROSE	(*flatly*) But independence, Lady Caroline, does snub the benevolences of others.
CAROLINE	I'm sorry about the beds. I gave no directions. I merely asked Costanza to remove them.
LOTTY	(*looking out*) It seems silly to be talking about beds in heaven.
CAROLINE	It is lovely, isn't it?
LOTTY	It's as if you belonged here all along.
CAROLINE	What do you mean?
LOTTY	In a setting as beautiful as yourself.
	(CAROLINE *smiles.* ROSE *frowns.*)
ROSE	Beauty is a gift.
CAROLINE	Yes.
ROSE	I hope you make the most of it, Lady Caroline.
CAROLINE	I've been making the most of it ever since I can remember.
ROSE	Good. Because it won't last.

(CAROLINE *quiets, looks down, rises.*)

CAROLINE   Please tell Mrs Graves that I don't care to take breakfast now. I'd like to go into the village.

(*She starts to exit into the garden.*)

LOTTY   (a *little hurt*) Oh. Hurry back, then.

CAROLINE   (*stopping – to* LOTTY) I am glad you've arrived safely. (*She exits.* ROSE *watches after her.* LOTTY *looks around.*)

LOTTY   Oh, Rose. We haven't been punished. We've been blessed!

ROSE   She's treading on the periwinkles.

LOTTY   They're hers as much as ours.

ROSE   It doesn't seem right.

LOTTY   One mustn't question in heaven. It isn't done.

ROSE   We've been displaced as hostesses.

LOTTY   None of us is the hostess. Here we are equal. (*She closes her eyes and takes a deep breath.*) Smell the fragrance, Rose. It's positively . . . sensual!

ROSE   Lotty!

LOTTY   It makes me want to kiss someone! (LOTTY *takes* ROSE'S *hand and kisses it.*) You know who would love all of this?

ROSE   Who? (LOTTY *thinks, frowns.*)

LOTTY   Never mind.

(*From within the house, the sound of* MRS GRAVES *furiously ringing her bell. The ladies shudder.*)

ROSE   That woman!

LOTTY   Mrs Graves doesn't know yet that she's in
                heaven. Oh, take it in, Rose! (*Shouting to the
                skies.*) Paradiso! (*To* ROSE, *beaming.*) Our first
                day in heaven! (MRS GRAVES' *bell rings.*) And
                Gabriel here to greet us! (*She runs into the
                villa.*) Paradiso!

                (ROSE *looks out, uncertain. She says a tiny
                prayer, closes her eyes and takes a deep,
                sensual breath. Something within her stirs.
                For the first time, she truly smiles. The church
                bell rings. Lights down.*)

                           Scene Two

*Lights up on the terrace at San Salvatore, nine days later.
Towels thrown about.* MRS GRAVES *sits at the table, hatless,
face to the sun, sleeping.* COSTANZA *enters from the villa with a
tray of tea and unshelled nuts, humming a tune gaily.*

COSTANZA   Buon giorno, Signora Graves. *[Good day.]*
                (MRS GRAVES *doesn't hear. She continues to
                hum, then suddenly shouts.*) Tè?! *[Tea!]*

MRS GRAVES   (*jumping*) Ah! Yes! Yes. (*Opens her parasol
                and composes herself.*) Have you found the
                cracker yet?

COSTANZA   (*serving tea*) "Cracker," Signora?

MRS GRAVES   The nutcracker. For the nuts.

COSTANZA   (*nodding*) Ah, sì, sì, "thee cracker." No.
                (*Offering cream. Teasingly.*) Latte?

MRS GRAVES   (*with great patience*) Thank you.

                (COSTANZA *pours.*)

COSTANZA   (*like a goat*) Ba-a-a-a-a.

                (*She exits.* MRS GRAVES *looks at the tea
                suspiciously.* CAROLINE *enters, sees* MRS
                GRAVES, *tries to exit again, but is caught.*)

MRS GRAVES   Ah! Lady Caroline. There is tea if you like.
                More than a week now and it's still the only
                thing Costanza appears capable of preparing.
                There hasn't been a meal served yet that did
                not present some sort of primitive challenge.
                Although I am not at all certain why I bother. I
                am the only one in this party who arrives
                promptly for meals. Or arrives at all, for that
                matter. I spent breakfast quite alone.

CAROLINE   (*taking tea*) That must have given you plenty
                of time to sit and remember.

MRS GRAVES   Remembrance and digestion should never be
                performed simultaneously.

                (ROSE *enters. Her appearance has changed
                considerably. She is dressed in a white summer
                dress, with her hair down, tied in the back.
                But she has been crying.*)

ROSE   Ladies.

CAROLINE   Hello.

MRS GRAVES   Ah, Mrs Arnott. You neglected breakfast.

ROSE   Have you seen Mrs Wilton, Lady Caroline?

CAROLINE   Yes. She took the boat out.

MRS GRAVES   Took the boat?

CAROLINE   The small rowing boat. She has quite a strong
                arm, our Lotty.

                (ROSE *eyes* CAROLINE.)

MRS GRAVES	Of that I have no doubt.
CAROLINE	Are you all right?
ROSE	All of these flowers make my eyes water a little.
MRS GRAVES	(*to* ROSE) That is a lovely frock you're wearing.
ROSE	(*sighing cynically*) Except for what, Mrs Graves?
MRS GRAVES	Sorry?
ROSE	You've nothing more to add?
MRS GRAVES	No. Why?
CAROLINE	You've just complimented someone, Mrs Graves.
MRS GRAVES	(*dumbfounded*) Oh.

(LOTTY *enters from the garden in a swimming outfit, barefooted, breathless, beaming. She has gone wild from head to toe, flowers in hand and in her flowing hair.*)

LOTTY	Good day, everyone!
ROSE	Hello, Lotty.
MRS GRAVES	Good Lord.
CAROLINE	Lotty! You look brilliant!
LOTTY	I feel brilliant, Lady Caroline! This has been the most glorious morning! Mrs Graves, doesn't it all just make you want to burst?
MRS GRAVES	I have never had a desire to burst.
LOTTY	(*drying herself with a towel*) I am famished! Is luncheon nearly ready?

ROSE	I believe so.
MRS GRAVES	Not macaroni again?
ROSE	Yes.
MRS GRAVES	(*with distainful regret*) From the land of Donatello.
LOTTY	Will you be joining us for luncheon today, Lady Caroline?
CAROLINE	(*visibly annoyed that she is now surrounded*) No, thank you. (*She begins to exit into the villa.*) I . . . I have a headache. Excuse me. (*She exits.*)
ROSE	What is the Italian for aspirin? (*She gets her phrase book.*)
MRS GRAVES	The remedy for headache is castor oil.
LOTTY	She doesn't have a headache.
MRS GRAVES	Carlyle suffered at one point terribly from headache . . .
LOTTY	She doesn't have a headache. She only wants to be left alone.
MRS GRAVES	Something else you've "seen", Mrs Wilton?
LOTTY	Yes. When I looked at her just now, I saw inside of her.
MRS GRAVES	I think I may burst after all.
LOTTY	San Salvatore is working its charms on Lady Caroline. (*Sneaking up behind* MRS GRAVES *and placing a flower in her hair, which* MRS GRAVES *doesn't notice.*) It's working its charms on all of us. Just at different rates, that's all. You really must take the boat out. Both of you.

I've never felt so calm, or been able to think so clearly.

MRS GRAVES   I think quite clearly enough, thank you.

LOTTY   And I've never wept so. A boat is a lovely place for weeping.

(MRS GRAVES *has had enough.*)

MRS GRAVES   (*rising*) I've castor oil in my room. (*She starts to exit.*) Mrs Wilton, if you were a woman of greater age, your behavior could be understood as dotage.

(LOTTY *considers.*)

LOTTY   Well, if I did have a choice, Mrs Graves, I suppose I would prefer dotage to condescension. (MRS GRAVES *stops, glares.*)

MRS GRAVES   Cover your legs! (*She exits.*)

LOTTY   (*inhales, looks about*) Isn't it gorgeous to be part of this all, Rose? The dandelions and the lilies, me and Mrs Graves . . . all let in, all welcome!

ROSE   (*at wit's end*) Honestly, Lotty. You'd make Pollyanna ill.

LOTTY   I can't help it. For the first time I feel such a part of everything!

ROSE   And what about me?

LOTTY   You must open yourself to it, Rose. You're angry.

ROSE   (*strongly*) Yes. I am.

LOTTY   That's good!

ROSE   You're all so independent.

LOTTY	Perhaps you don't want to be independent.
ROSE	I do!
LOTTY	Nine days without husbands. Perhaps that doesn't suit you, Rose. I have a confession myself. Since we arrived here there hasn't been one moment when I wasn't thinking of Mellersh.
ROSE	I dreamed of him last night.
LOTTY	Mellersh?
ROSE	Frederick.
LOTTY	"Frederick." So that's his name!
ROSE	And I forgot to say my prayers.
LOTTY	Your dream was your prayer.
ROSE	*That* . . . is not what one prays for.
LOTTY	Physical love, you mean?
ROSE	Lotty! Mrs Graves is right. Sometimes you are too much.
LOTTY	I can't help it, Rose. I don't know how else to be.
ROSE	It's selfish.
LOTTY	I am a particular challenge. As much as Mrs Graves. And as much as poor Mellersh.
ROSE	Poor Mellersh? Are you hearing yourself?
LOTTY	Yes, I hear myself. Waking every morning to that second bed staring at me. I've been a miser, Rose. Rationing my love.

ROSE   What are you saying?

LOTTY   We must forgive our husbands, and ourselves, and get on with things.

ROSE   Lotty . . .

(LOTTY *takes a deep breath.*)

LOTTY   I've written to Mellersh and told him everything.

ROSE   What?!

LOTTY   Well, except about my nest egg. I wish he were here so I could tell him that as well.

ROSE   You don't mean that.

LOTTY   I do, Rose. (*Nervously.*) I've . . . invited him.

ROSE   (*aghast*) You can't be serious.

LOTTY   We said in London that there would be room for guests.

ROSE   We said in London that there would be an extra room.

LOTTY   (*becoming increasingly excited*) And there is! There's room for everyone! Even your Frederick.

ROSE   Frederick?

LOTTY   Do you call him "Freddy"?

ROSE   I do not. (*Becoming increasingly upset.*) The whole idea of our coming here was to get away.

LOTTY   We got away!

ROSE   And now, after barely one week of it, you want to ask the very people . . .

LOTTY	The very people we were getting away from. It's true. It's idiotically illogical. But they must be here now. I've seen it!
ROSE	Stop this, Lotty. I'm warning you.
LOTTY	Write to your Frederick, Rose, and tell him everything!
ROSE	It's not that simple.
LOTTY	About San Salvatore . . . and the wisteria . . .
ROSE	You can't understand . . .
	(LOTTY *laughs.*)
LOTTY	And Mrs Graves, and . . .
ROSE	(*desperately*) LISTEN TO ME! He wouldn't come!
LOTTY	Don't be silly.
ROSE	I lost a child, Lotty. I lost my child. Our child.
LOTTY	(*Quietly.*) Oh, Rose.
ROSE	It's been two years now, but . . .
LOTTY	No . . .
ROSE	Two years of trying to understand such a . . . punishment.
LOTTY	(*going to* ROSE, *holding her*) No. No. (ROSE *embraces her, crying.*) Rose. (*Thinks.*) I can't pretend to know what you're feeling, Rose. But I do know that you are not alone.
ROSE	I have you now.
LOTTY	Not me. Frederick.

Rose   You're not listening.

Lotty   You must invite him.

Rose   He won't come.

Lotty   He will. I've seen it! Frederick and Mellersh. At
                San Salvatore.

                (Rose *smiles.*)

Rose   How can you see Frederick, Lotty? You don't
                know a thing about him.

Lotty   You're such a damned logical woman, Mrs
                Arnott. (Lotty *extends her hand.*) Come. Let
                me take you boating. You can tell me
                everything.

Rose   You said you were hungry.

Lotty   We'll pick berries. You're right, Rose. I haven't
                been listening. But we're sisters, remember?
                And I'm listening now.

                (Rose *takes* Lotty's *hand. They exit into the
                garden.* Caroline *enters from the villa, sees
                them leaving, sighs, relieved. She goes to the
                chaise, retrieves a flask from behind the
                pillows, opens it, drinks, exhales deeply.* Mrs
                Graves *enters from the villa, flower in hair
                and castor oil in hand. She watches* Caroline
                replace the flask.)

Mrs Graves   Castor oil! (Caroline *smoothes herself.*) I
                expect the sun has caused you to feel ill. You
                should take some castor oil and go to bed.

Caroline   But I don't want castor oil, and I don't want to
                go to bed. I just want to be alone to think.

Mrs Graves   No one wants a woman who thinks. You should
                go to bed and get well.

CAROLINE   I am well.

MRS GRAVES   Then I have had all the trouble of coming after
                you for nothing.

CAROLINE   Wouldn't you prefer coming after me and
                finding me well to coming after me and finding
                me ill?

                (MRS GRAVES *lets out a small laugh, walks into
                the sun and looks up, inhales deeply.*
                COSTANZA *enters with a telegram.*)

COSTANZA   Un telegramma, per Signora Wilton. *[A
                telegram, for Mrs Wilton.]*

CAROLINE   È nel giardino, Costanza. *[She is in the
                garden.]*

COSTANZA   Ah. Grazie, Donna Carolina. (*She exits into the
                garden, calling.*) Signora Wilton! Un
                telegramma! Signora Wilton!

MRS GRAVES   Now who could be sending Mrs Wilton a
                telegram?

CAROLINE   You shouldn't be so hard on Lotty, Mrs
                Graves.

MRS GRAVES   That woman must be curbed.

CAROLINE   She understands things, I think, in her way.

MRS GRAVES   She "sees" things, you mean. Just a moment
                ago she said she saw inside of you.

CAROLINE   If that's so, then she's one of the few people
                who has ever bothered.

MRS GRAVES   (*considering*) You are an intriguing creature,
                Lady Caroline. I am very glad there are no men
                about. You are precisely the sort of woman who

unbalances men. My mother unbalanced men, and I dare say it can come at quite a cost.

CAROLINE   Pricey, was she? (MRS GRAVES *glares*.) I apologize, Mrs Graves. Sometimes I can go too far.

MRS GRAVES   I understand some things myself, Lady Caroline, in my way. The burden of wit on our sex, for example. You should be thankful for your beauty. At least you are allowed credit for that.

CAROLINE   I would gladly trade it all, Mrs Graves.

MRS GRAVES   (*chuckling*) For what?

CAROLINE   Things lost.

MRS GRAVES   How so?

CAROLINE   Jolly war, wasn't it? Except for those who never returned. And those of us who loved them.

              (MRS GRAVES *softens*.)

MRS GRAVES   A brother?

CAROLINE   Never mind.

MRS GRAVES   You are impossible.

CAROLINE   A husband.

MRS GRAVES   A husband? I . . . (*Moved*.) I am sorry . . . I didn't know.

CAROLINE   No one did. We secretly married the night before his duty. For good luck. Funny, no?

MRS GRAVES   I . . . I am very surprised you've told me this, Lady Caroline.

CAROLINE   You have such a warm way of drawing people in, Mrs Graves.

MRS GRAVES   I grieved terribly when I lost my Clayton. That came as quite a surprise, I must say. Not nearly as surprising as it would have been to him.

CAROLINE   I had a reputation to uphold. I danced instead.

MRS GRAVES   You've not found another?

CAROLINE   Another? We are the "moderns" now, Mrs Graves. There's always another. When the wine has been spilt, there's still the dregs. Artists who want to "mold" me, photographers who want to "capture" me. And writers . . . well, what woman wouldn't want to be studied, annotated, indexed?

MRS GRAVES   They adore you, I'm sure.

CAROLINE   They don't even know me.

MRS GRAVES   Are you certain that's their fault?

                (CAROLINE *softens*.)

CAROLINE   To be fair, there is one. Are you familiar with Florian Ayers?

                (MRS GRAVES *shudders*.)

MRS GRAVES   Florian Ayers? That writer?!

CAROLINE   Mother's latest social acquisition.

MRS GRAVES   "Romantic biographies."

CAROLINE   Indeed.

MRS GRAVES   Salacious!

CAROLINE   And wildly successful.

MRS GRAVES   Good God. (*Thinks.*) I once had a dog that chased his own tail.

CAROLINE   And?

MRS GRAVES   People praised him, too.

CAROLINE   But Florian is sweet, really. And sad somehow. A lost soulmate, perhaps. (MRS GRAVES *thinks, stirred.*)

MRS GRAVES   A lost soulmate. I feel so restless today.

CAROLINE   You've gotten some sun, Mrs Graves. (MRS GRAVES *retrieves her parasol, starts to open it.*) It becomes you.

              (MRS GRAVES *smiles, closes the parasol.* LOTTY *lets out a great yelp from the garden.*)

LOTTY   (*offstage*) Mrs Graves! Lady Caroline!

MRS GRAVES   Lady Caroline. About the cognac.

LOTTY   (*offstage*) Paradiso!

MRS GRAVES   Don't trade everything for that.

              (LOTTY *enters from the garden excitedly, with* ROSE *and* COSTANZA, *who have been dressed in flowers.*)

LOTTY   Paradiso, Lady Caroline! Paradiso, Mrs Graves!

MRS GRAVES   Good God!

LOTTY   Ladies. Ladies.

CAROLINE   What is it, Lotty?

LOTTY   It's wonderful, that's what it is! I'm sorry that this is without warning, but . . . I am having a visitor!

MRS GRAVES   What?!

CAROLINE   A visitor? But we came here to escape people,
              Lotty.

LOTTY   Yes, I know. But I don't want to escape him
              now.

CAROLINE   Him?

MRS GRAVES   A man?!

LOTTY   Yes, a man. Mr Wilton!

MRS GRAVES   A relative?

LOTTY   A husband!

MRS GRAVES   Mrs Wilton, if this is another one of your
              ghosts . . .

LOTTY   No, Mrs Graves. It's my husband! In the flesh!
              (*Lifting the telegram.*) He left London last
              night!

MRS GRAVES   But you are a widow!

ROSE   She never said anything of the kind, Mrs
              Graves.

LOTTY   Lady Caroline, I'll need your help with
              Costanza to prepare the spare room and then . . .

MRS GRAVES   (*increasingly irate*) One moment! Am I to
              understand that you are proposing to reserve
              the one unoccupied bedroom in the castle for
              the exclusive use of your family?

CAROLINE   Yes, why the spare room if he's your husband,
              Lotty?

LOTTY   Oh, no. If I share my room with Mellersh, I risk
              losing all I'm feeling. Don't you see?

CAROLINE	(*laughing*) Actually, I do! By all means, let's give Mr Wilton the spare room, Mrs Graves. Any other arrangement would be scandalous!
LOTTY	Thank you, Caroline. And Rose is going to write to her husband.
MRS GRAVES	Another husband?!
LOTTY	Aren't you, Rose?
ROSE	Yes. I am!
MRS GRAVES	Is anyone here who they claimed to be?
CAROLINE	But there is only one spare room.
LOTTY	Oh, Rose won't mind sharing her room with her husband. It's written all over her.
	(ROSE *gasps, tries to grab* LOTTY, *but she runs.* CAROLINE *laughs.*)
MRS GRAVES	Husbands were not part of our agreement, Mrs Arnott. You must not write to him.
ROSE	As you wish, Mrs Graves. (*Gathering strength.*) I'll telegraph him!
MRS GRAVES	Oh! Well . . . I am going to invite a guest!
ROSE	Who, Mrs Graves? Tennyson or Carlyle?
	(LOTTY *gasps.* MRS GRAVES *burns.*)
MRS GRAVES	Kate Lumley! (*The ladies laugh louder.*) There is nothing funny about Kate Lumley, I assure you. I shall write to her this instant, and she shall have the spare room! There are to be no men roaming San Salvatore as long as I am staying here. Kate Lumley will see to that!
	(WILDING *enters from the villa.*)

WILDING   Cheers, everyone!

MRS GRAVES   (*appalled*) Oh!

LOTTY   (*thrilled*) Mr Wilding!

WILDING   Is this a bad time? I was passing through to
               Rome and thought I'd see how things were
               going.

LOTTY   This is too much!

MRS GRAVES   I should say! (*She rings her bell furiously.*)

CAROLINE   (*noticeably impressed*) You may remember my
               letter, Mr Wilding. (*Lifts her hand.*) Lady
               Caroline Bramble.

               (WILDING *nods, looks to* ROSE *excitedly.*)

WILDING   Mrs Arnott! (*He goes to* ROSE, *takes her hand,
               spins her around.*) And you wore white!

ROSE   (*beaming*) Mr Wilding!

WILDING   It's just as I saw it!

LOTTY   It's just as *I* saw it!

               (COSTANZA *enters, sees* WILDING.)

COSTANZA   Tonio! (*She runs to* WILDING. *They embrace.*)

WILDING   Costanza!

COSTANZA   Bambino mio! *[My baby boy!]*

MRS GRAVES   Oh, good God!

COSTANZA   (*to* WILDING, *pointing at* MRS GRAVES) Pazza!
               (*Miming horns.*) Diabolica! *[Crazy!
               Diabolical!]*

WILDING   All my ladies!

CAROLINE   (*snubbed*) Well.

WILDING   At San Salvatore!

MRS GRAVES   Really!

WILDING   And this must be the Mrs Graves you told me of . . .

MRS GRAVES   (*furiously*) Mr Wilding!

WILDING   For whom I've carried, all the way from London, a bag of the finest English walnuts . . . (*He holds out a ribboned bag.* MRS GRAVES' *eyes widen.*) . . . which I shall gladly trade for a few hours in your lovely company, and the promise of hearing your golden memories of the great Lord Tennyson.

                (MRS GRAVES *opens her mouth, but is wordless. She slowly smiles, then coquettishly takes the bag.*)

MRS GRAVES   (*bubbling over*) Make yourself at home!

                (*Lights down.*)

Scene Three

Lights up on the terrace of San Salvatore, the following afternoon. ROSE *sits on the chaise in a summer dress, hair loose, with parasol, posing for* WILDING, *who stands before a canvas and easel, sketching her.*

WILDING   That's it. And just a little . . . there. Would you lift your chin just a . . . (*She does so.*) Yes. You have a fine chin, Mrs Arnott. And now it is . . . caught. I must say you have shown admirable patience.

ROSE   I hope that won't be the tone of the portrait, Mr Wilding.

WILDING   Oh?

ROSE   I should hate to one day find myself used in
                 textbooks as an illustration of "admirable
                 patience."

                 (COSTANZA *enters from the villa with tea.*)

COSTANZA   Tè.

WILDING   (*not looking up from his work*) Grazie,
                 Costanza.

                 (COSTANZA *sees* ROSE.)

COSTANZA   Ah! Squisita! Bellissima! *[Lovely! Beautiful!]*

ROSE   Is that good?

WILDING   Quite.

COSTANZA   (*looking at the sketch*) Oh, Tonio.
                 Meravigliosa! *[Marvelous.]*

WILDING   Vi ricorda qualquno, Costanza? *[Does she
                 remind you of anyone?]*

COSTANZA   Mi ricorda? *[Remind me?]* (*Thinks, realizes,
                 sadly.*) Ah, sì. Lo vedo. *[Yes, I see it.]*
                 (*Changing the subject.*) Ma quando dipingerai
                 il ritratto di Costanza? *[But when are you
                 going to paint Costanza's portrait?]* (*She
                 poses.*)

WILDING   Ho già fatto! Troppo difettoso non posso
                 mostrarlo in pubblico. *[I have! Too bad I can't
                 show them in public.]*

COSTANZA   Eh? (*Realizes he's teasing, laughs,
                 embarrassed.*) Oh tu! Diabolino! Tu set il figlio
                 del tuo papa, non c'è dubbio! *[Oh, you! Little
                 devil! You are your father's boy, no doubt*

about it!] (Exiting into the villa.) Set il figlio
di papa! *[Your father's boy.]*

ROSE   *(still posing)* Costanza is very fond of you.

WILDING   Oh, yes. Part of the family. Part of *her* family, I
              mean. Costanza is the mother of nine.

ROSE   Nine?!

WILDING   Ten, counting me now, I suppose.

ROSE   Speaking of admirable patience.

WILDING   I owe Costanza a great deal. She was wonderful
              with Mother. Here . . . you've worked enough.
              Let's have some tea.

              *(WILDING pours tea and prepares a small plate
              of biscuits. ROSE stands, stretches. She's
              unusually relaxed. She motions toward the
              sketch.)*

ROSE   May I?

WILDING   Of course. *(She takes a look.)* Mind you, it's
              only a sketch.

ROSE   *(moved)* It's lovely, Mr Wilding.

WILDING   I shall finish it properly in Rome. *(ROSE smiles,
              walks to the tea.)*

ROSE   Rome must be fascinating.

WILDING   *(handing her a cup of tea)* Very beautiful. Very
              romantic. And one must have one's escape,
              mustn't one? *(They are close. ROSE smells the
              tea.)*

ROSE   Cinnamon.

WILDING   "Cannella."

ROSE   Cannella.

WILDING   Sì. Biscotto? (*He offers her the plate of
                biscuits.*)

ROSE   (*blushing*) Grazie. (*She takes the plate.*) Is Mrs
                Wilton still out?

WILDING   Yes. Well, out again, that is. She and Mrs
                Graves went to the village.

ROSE   To the village? Mrs Graves?

WILDING   Does that surprise you?

ROSE   I suppose yesterday it would have. But since
                you've arrived, Mr Wilding, we seem to have a
                somewhat altered Mrs Graves.

WILDING   Really? I find her most delightful.

ROSE   You've doted on her properly. You've doted on
                us all.

WILDING   Sometimes all it takes is a little attention to do
                the trick. (*Looking at her.*) You must admit,
                Mrs Arnott, that I was correct about
                something.

ROSE   What?

WILDING   That you were meant to be at San Salvatore.

ROSE   (*thoroughly, pleasantly embarrassed*) You and
                Costanza just now . . .

WILDING   Yes?

ROSE   Were you comparing me with the original?

                (WILDING *is stunned.*)

WILDING   The . . . what?

                (ROSE *senses she's said something wrong.*)

ROSE   The portrait of the Madonna? Above the
            stairs?

WILDING   (*relieved*) Oh. Yes. You have to admit the
            likeness is extraordinary.

ROSE   I didn't know I looked so solemn.

WILDING   You don't. Not today.

ROSE   I don't think my vicar would approve of such
            comparisons.

WILDING   No, no. But then that's what vicars do, don't
            they? (ROSE *smiles.* WILDING *looks at her.*)
            Actually, it's someone else you remind me of.

ROSE   Not some "old flame," I pray.

WILDING   Oh, no, no. Nothing of that nature. (WILDING
            thinks. ROSE *becomes a little uncertain, but
            smiles inquisitively.*) There are moments, Mrs
            Arnott, when you remind me so much of my
            mother.

            (*Total silence.* ROSE *keeps her composure.
            Except for the biscuits, which spill onto the
            floor.*)

ROSE   Oh!

WILDING   Oh, dear. (*He picks up the biscuits and takes
            the plate.*) Here, I'll get you more.

ROSE   No, no. (*She looks out as* WILDING *busies with
            the biscuits, catches her breath, thinks.*) I
            know you were very close to your mother, Mr
            Wilding. So it's very nice of you to say such a
            thing.

WILDING   I saw it the first time we met.

ROSE   I see. Are there any photographs of her here?

WILDING   I wish there were. Mother was much too
             modest for that. Father and I both tried, but
             she'd have none of it, I'm afraid.

ROSE   And what was your father like, Mr Wilding?

WILDING   Father? Father loved beauty. He loved life. He
             lived life. Mother was always a little
             embarrassed by that, I think. A shame, really.
             Because she *was* his life. He flat out adored
             her.

ROSE   Sweet.

WILDING   (*looking out, pointing*) Do you see that acacia
             tree there? (ROSE *looks out.*) Father told a story
             that his father, my grandfather, while walking
             one day with my grandmother, thrust his
             walking stick into the ground at that spot and
             said, "Here we shall have an acacia." He left
             the stick in the ground as a reminder, and
             presently, how long afterward nobody seems to
             remember, the stick began to sprout. And it
             was an acacia. (ROSE *smiles.*) After duty, in
             hospital, I tried to paint that tree, but could
             never do it justice.

ROSE   Were you wounded?

WILDING   Just . . . a bit tired. I came straight from
             hospital to San Salvatore, in fact. And mother
             and Costanza.

ROSE   I'm sure that cured you.

             (WILDING *smiles, sadly.* LOTTY *yells from the
             garden.*)

LOTTY   (*offstage*) Yoo Hoo!

WILDING   Here they are.

ROSE   They look as if they've bought the whole
             place!

(LOTTY *enters from the garden with* MRS GRAVES *on her arm.* MRS GRAVES' *mode of dress has lightened.* LOTTY *is bright and well-groomed. They are laden with packages, with which* WILDING *helps.*)

LOTTY   We're almost there, Mrs Graves.

MRS GRAVES   Good God, you've been saying that for an hour.

LOTTY   And now it's true! Thank you, Mr Wilding.

WILDING   I should have gone along, ladies.

LOTTY   Oh, no. We made much progress on our own, didn't we, Mrs Graves?

MRS GRAVES   We march on Rome tomorrow.

LOTTY   We are in for a treat, everyone!

MRS GRAVES   Well, I make no promises, but I have at least procured the makings of a proper meal. Tonight I shall teach Costanza how to prepare steak and kidney pie.

LOTTY   Rose, perhaps you'd help me with Costanza. There's teaching to be done!

ROSE   Yes. (LOTTY *and* ROSE *gather the packages.*)

WILDING   Shall I have Costanza bring tea inside?

MRS GRAVES   (*sweetly*) I should like to take my tea out here with you, Mr Wilding.

WILDING   Very well.

LOTTY   Thank you for a grand time, Mrs Graves. (*She kisses* MRS GRAVES *on the cheek, exits.* MRS GRAVES *is aghast.*)

ROSE   And thank you, Mr Wilding. For everything.

WILDING   I haven't done anything, Mrs Arnott.

ROSE   (*sincerely*) You have. (*She exits.*)

MRS GRAVES   Mr Wilding, I would like tonight's dinner to be
                my thanks for your generous company. I am
                sorry you are leaving tomorrow. It is so nice to
                have a man about the place.

WILDING   I'm glad San Salvatore agrees with you, Mrs
                Graves.

MRS GRAVES   How could it not? You are very young to be a
                man of property.

WILDING   I can hardly take credit for that.

MRS GRAVES   But you should. Inheritance is so much more
                respectable than acquisition.

WILDING   How did you fare in the village?

MRS GRAVES   Oh, that Mrs Wilton is a stubborn thing. From
                day one I have tried to make peace with her,
                but to no avail.

WILDING   With some people there seems to be no choice
                but to relent.

MRS GRAVES   No! To relent is to surrender, Mr Wilding. That
                is not the English way at all. You have spent
                far too much time in Italy, I fear. (*She walks to
                the sketch.*)

WILDING   Perhaps you are right.

MRS GRAVES   This Mrs Arnott is a particular case herself.

WILDING   Yes.

MRS GRAVES   (*watching his reaction*) Yes. Tell me, Mr
                Wilding, what do you make of our Lady
                Caroline?

WILDING   She's lovely. I seem to have made a poor
               impression, however.

MRS GRAVES   There's more to Lady Caroline than meets the
               eye.

WILDING   She is very solitary.

MRS GRAVES   A common thing today, it seems, since the war.

WILDING   And you? I picture you in London surrounded
               by grandchildren.

MRS GRAVES   Grand . . . ? Oh no, no. One needs children to
               have grandchildren, Mr Wilding.

               (CAROLINE *enters.*)

WILDING   Ah! Lady Caroline.

MRS GRAVES   Who missed dinner again last night.

CAROLINE   I wasn't feeling well.

WILDING   I do hope you are feeling better.

MRS GRAVES   Our Lady Caroline has a remarkable inclination
               toward rapid recovery. (*She sits and places her
               stick aside.*)

CAROLINE   Mr Wilding. Since you are here, perhaps
               something can be done about the bath. It is
               really quite a confusion.

WILDING   (*cordially*) A confusion?

CAROLINE   One shouldn't have to risk one's life merely for
               the convenience of warm water.

WILDING   (*chuckling*) Oh yes, the heater. It is a rather
               ancient system. But really, there is no danger at
               all if done with just a little Italian patience. (*He
               and* MRS GRAVES *smile.*)

CAROLINE   (*coldly*) It is a danger, Mr Wilding. Am I
                understood?

WILDING   (*realising he has misspoken*) I shall look into
                the matter before my departure.

                (COSTANZA *enters from the villa, upset.*)

COSTANZA   Signora Graves?

MRS GRAVES   Ah! I am needed! (*She rises and heads toward
                the kitchen.*)

COSTANZA   (*pleadingly*) Tonio?

WILDING   (*seeing* COSTANZA'*s distress*) Sì, sì, Costanza.
                May I be of some help, Mrs Graves?

MRS GRAVES   Well . . . you could lure Mrs Wilton out here,
                so that I need not contend with her in the
                kitchen.

CAROLINE   Mrs Graves? (MRS GRAVES *stops. Slyly.*) Your
                stick.

                (MRS GRAVES *and* WILDING *look at the stick,
                which has been left behind.*)

MRS GRAVES   (*flustered*) Well. (WILDING *retrieves the stick,
                hands it to her.*) Imagine that. (*She exits into
                the villa.*)

WILDING   Lady Caroline, I am sorry about the bath. I do
                hope you'll join us this evening for dinner.

CAROLINE   (*flatly*) Do you?

WILDING   I do. Excuse me. (*He exits into the villa.
                COSTANZA enters and approaches CAROLINE,
                holds out a card.*)

COSTANZA   Un biglietto da visita, Donna Carolina. *[A
                visitor's card.]*

CAROLINE	Che? *[What?]* (*Reads the card, gasps.*) Good God!(*Laughs.*)
COSTANZA	È nell'entrata. *[He is in the entry way.]*
CAROLINE	Portalo qui, per favore, Costanza. *[Bring him out, please.]*
COSTANZA	Sì, sì, Signorina. (*Exits into the villa.* CAROLINE *readies herself.*)
CAROLINE	Well, now. (CONSTANZA *enters with* FREDERICK. *Turning on her charms.*) Florian Ayers!
FREDERICK	Ah! Caroline! I had no idea if I was at the right place.
CAROLINE	You naughty boy!
FREDERICK	(*with uncertain joviality*) Your mother told me where you were, and I was on my book tour anyhow, and so I thought I would look in and see how you were doing.
CAROLINE	I don't recall your book tour extending to Italy.
FREDERICK	Yes, well. It doesn't really. (*Weakly.*) But I was already in Lisbon . . .
CAROLINE	You are a wicked thing, Mr Ayers.
FREDERICK	No, no. Just weak, I'm told.
CAROLINE	Didn't mother tell you I was doing a rest cure?
FREDERICK	Yes, she did. That's why I haven't intruded on you earlier in the day. I thought you would probably sleep all day and get up just in time for tea. (*Crumbling.*) I couldn't help myself, Caroline.

(COSTANZA *clears her throat.*)

CAROLINE	Grazie, Costanza.
COSTANZA	(*skeptically*) Uno in più per cena? *[One more for dinner?]*
CAROLINE	Sì. Grazie. (COSTANZA *exits into the villa.*)
FREDERICK	What did you say?
CAROLINE	I told her to add you to dinner. (*Finding it difficult to maintain her carefree pose.*) Mother didn't send you, did she, Florian?
FREDERICK	Oh no, on my word, Caroline.
CAROLINE	I wanted to have a month that was perfectly blank.
FREDERICK	And now I've interrupted.
CAROLINE	(*sincerely*) I feel all a jumble.
FREDERICK	(*attempting again to lift the mood*) Perhaps it's good I came then! There's a jazz club in Genoa! I was given the name. Something "Eeny," "Leeny," "Cheeny." I'm told it's quite the thing!
CAROLINE	I'm so tired, Florian.
FREDERICK	(*uncomfortably*) *You*, Caroline? (*Seeing the sketch, deflecting.*) Have you taken up art now? (*He goes to the sketch, studies it, at first with pleasure, and then with utter bewilderment.*)
CAROLINE	I don't know what to do anymore.
FREDERICK	(*scratching his head, transfixed*) Nothing a little jazz and gin won't cure, is there? Speaking of which . . . (*Turning back to* CAROLINE, *dazed.*) I seem to be a little dry at the moment. Any "refreshments" hereabout?

CAROLINE	There's tea.
FREDERICK	(*disappointed*) Oh.
CAROLINE	Here. (*She retrieves the flask.*) This will help.
FREDERICK	There's my girl. (*He drinks, glances toward the sketch.* CAROLINE *thinks.*)
CAROLINE	(*sadly*) Florian? Have you ever lost hold of something? Something so vital that you didn't know how to go on?
	(FREDERICK *considers.*)
FREDERICK	(*sincerely*) I have.
CAROLINE	What did you do?
FREDERICK	I went on.
CAROLINE	But it's not the same.
FREDERICK	No.
CAROLINE	You've always seemed like someone I could talk to, Florian. There's something disarmingly . . . *honest* about you.
FREDERICK	(*dropping all pretense*) We *should* talk, Caroline. Perhaps we could find a restaurant in the village.
CAROLINE	Yes? Oh, but there's to be a special dinner here tonight.
FREDERICK	Well, we can make an early appearance and then go. Here. (*He hands her the flask.* CAROLINE *smiles, decides not to drink, closes the flask.*)
CAROLINE	(*indicating the chaise*) You lie down and rest a bit, then. Let me go change.
FREDERICK	I could do with a rest. (*Goes to the chaise.*) That's really quite a climb up from the village.

There was a motorcar at the station, but the driver was too busy arguing with some other chap. So many English in Italy this time of year.

CAROLINE   Well, rest, and then you can regale all of us at dinner with stories of your tour.

FREDERICK   "All of us"? I hope I'm not interrupting anything.

CAROLINE   Ladies.

FREDERICK   Ah!

(CAROLINE *starts to exit into the villa, stops.*)

CAROLINE   Tell me something. The jazz and the gin. Would you ever give it all up?

(FREDERICK *thinks, sighs.*)

FREDERICK   Gladly.

(CAROLINE *smiles, gives him a quick kiss, exits.* FREDERICK *looks around, relaxes back on the chaise, settles in, shuts his eyes, rests.* ROSE *enters from the villa, goes to the sketch, studies it.* FREDERICK *begins singing 'Ma, He's Making Eyes at Me" under his breath.* ROSE *looks up, sees him, freezes in disbelief. She walks to him.*)

ROSE   Frederick?

FREDERICK   (*dreaming*) Rose?

ROSE   Frederick? (FREDERICK *opens his eyes, stares.*)

FREDERICK   Rose? (*He jumps up, amazed at her appearance, stunned by her presence.*) Rose! (ROSE *throws her arms around him, kissing him passionately.* COSTANZA *enters, sees, crosses herself, exits.*)

ROSE	Frederick! Oh, Frederick! When did you start?
FREDERICK	(*trying to decipher between kisses*) Start?
ROSE	Yes. When did you leave?
FREDERICK	(*attempting an acceptable answer, weakly*) Yesterday morning?
ROSE	The very instant then!
FREDERICK	Yes! The very instant!
ROSE	How quickly my telegram must have got to Lisbon!
FREDERICK	(*understanding*) Telegram! Yes, yes, didn't it though!
ROSE	Oh, Frederick! Frederick! (*She kisses him fully. WILDING enters from the villa, sees.*)
WILDING	Well, I'm damned.
ROSE	Oh! Oh, Mr Wilding! Mr Wilding. Forgive me. I'm so embarrassed.
WILDING	No, no.
ROSE	(*to* FREDERICK) This is Mr Frederick, Wilding ... (*Laughs. To* WILDING.) Oh ... I mean, this is Mr Arnott, Frederick. (*Laughs, composes herself.*) Mr Wilding, this ... (*Smiles.*) ... is my husband ... *Mister* Arnott.
FREDERICK	How ... how do you do? (*They shake hands.*)
WILDING	I'm not quite sure, really.
ROSE	Mr Wilding owns the castle, Frederick.
FREDERICK	(*wide-eyed, ready to say anything*) Ah! Beautiful!

WILDING   Yes.

ROSE   (*giddily*) Oh, Frederick. I didn't know whether
               to write or not, whether you wanted . . . but
               Lotty made me believe!

FREDERICK   Oh, well, Lotty, yes. Who's Lotty?

ROSE   Lotty! Mrs Wilton. One of the other guests.
               She's from Hampstead as well. And, oh, there's
               Mrs Graves. I don't know what you'll make of
               her. And Lady Caroline Bramble!

FREDERICK   (*weakly*) Really? Lady Caroline Bramble?

WILDING   If you'll excuse me . . .

ROSE   (*choosing her words as discreetly* as *possible,
               trying to hide her excitement, gathering*
               FREDERICK'S *things*) Oh, no. If you'll be so kind
               enough to excuse *us*, Mr Wilding, I think it
               would be best if Mr Arnott and myself retired
               presently to our room to . . . prepare for dinner.

WILDING   Right. Right, then. A pleasure meeting you, Mr
               Arnott.

FREDERICK   Likewise.

ROSE   Oh, Frederick! (*Taking his hand and leading
               him toward the villa.*) Lotty always said we
               must believe that anything can happen. And it
               can!

FREDERICK   (*flummoxed*) Yes. Apparently it can!

               (*They exit.* COSTANZA *enters from the villa,
               holds out a card.*)

COSTANZA   Tonio! Un altro! *[Another!]*

WILDING   Un altro? (*He takes the card. A newly humbled*
               MELLERSH *timidly enters from the villa, in hat*

*and coat, clutching his travel bag and Italian
phrase book.*) Buon giorno.

MELLERSH   (*attempting Italian, badly*) Bu-on gi-or-no. Par
            . . . parla . . . Ing . . . Ing . . . *[Do you speak
            English?]*

WILDING   Inglese? Not only do I speak English, I am
            English.

MELLERSH   Ah! Thank heavens! (*He hands his things to
            COSTANZA.*) Mellersh Wilton, family solicitor.

WILDING   So it says. Antony Wilding. (*They shake
            hands.*)

MELLERSH   How do you do?

WILDING   You are a relative of our Mrs Wilton?

MELLERSH   You could say that. (*Looking about.
            Completely out of his element.*) Then my wife
            is here?

WILDING   (*perplexed*) Who?

MELLERSH   Mrs Wilton.

WILDING   (*stunned*) Your wife?! Yes, yes. She's just in
            the kitchen with Mrs Graves. (*To himself.*) Now
            she's a widow, surely. (*Composing himself.*)
            Costanza, prenda Signora Wilton, prego. *[Get
            Mrs Wilton.]*

COSTANZA   (*at wit's end*) Sì, Tonio. Quanti sono per cena
            adesso? *[How many for dinner now?]*

WILDING   Sette. A meno che non ci aspettino altre
            sorprese. *[Seven. Unless there are even more
            surprises.]*

COSTANZA   Sì, sì. È'una sopresa dopo l'altra! *[It's just one
            surprise after another.]*

	(*She exits, pointedly leaving* MELLERSH'S *things.*)
WILDING	Costanza will fetch her for you. You look parched. Would you like some tea?
MELLERSH	Oh, Please!
WILDING	(*serving*) Any trouble finding the place?
MELLERSH	A struggle or two, but I rallied.
WILDING	You're familiar with Italy?
MELLERSH	(*weakly*) I've read books. (*Takes the tea, drinks.*) Thank you. (*Assessing* WILDING, *uncomfortably.*) My wife wrote that this was a party of four ladies.
WILDING	Yes.
	(MELLERSH *waits.*)
MELLERSH	And you?
WILDING	I suppose I'm what you'd call the landlord.
MELLERSH	You mean you are the owner of the place?
WILDING	Yes.
MELLERSH	Oh? (*Pleased.*) Oh! My wife also wrote that Lady Caroline Bramble was among the guests.
WILDING	Yes.
MELLERSH	(*even more pleased*) Well! (LOTTY *enters from the villa.*)
LOTTY	(*softly*) Hello, Mellersh.
	(MELLERSH *grins, turns, but turns away again and composes himself.*)
MELLERSH	Mrs Wilton.

(*A nervous moment.* LOTTY *is ready to burst, and she does. She rushes toward* MELLERSH.)

LOTTY   Oh, Mellersh! Welcome!

(MELLERSH *jumps. His tea cup flies from its saucer and is caught by* WILDING.)

MELLERSH Good heavens, Charlotte!

LOTTY   Have you and Mr Wilding introduced yourselves?

MELLERSH Surely.

LOTTY   Are you all right, Mr Wilding?

WILDING   (*dazed*) What? Oh, no . . . I mean yes! Fine, fine. (*He returns the cup to its saucer.*) I suppose I should go check on the steak and kidney pie. (*To himself, exiting.*) Widows!

LOTTY   I am so glad to see you, Mellersh!

MELLERSH Really? But you couldn't meet me at the station?

LOTTY   Oh, but I had so much to do! And the time . . . well, San Salvatore has a way of making one forget all about time.

MELLERSH (*attempting control*) Forget about time? Absurd.

LOTTY   It's not absurd. You'll see.

MELLERSH I would like to pay my respects to your hostess, Charlotte.

LOTTY   Hostess?

MELLERSH This "Mrs Arnott" who invited you here.

LOTTY	There is something I haven't told you, Mellersh.
MELLERSH	There appear to be many things you haven't told me.
LOTTY	(*nervously*) I . . . wasn't invited here.
MELLERSH	Not . . . ? You named three ladies in your telegram.
LOTTY	Yes. The four of us are here.
MELLERSH	And this Mr Wilding.
LOTTY	I know it must seem confusing, Mellersh, and it should to you, and for that I do apologize. But, you see . . . it's just that the four of us ladies, we . . . well . . . we have rented the castle.
MELLERSH	Rented?
LOTTY	Yes. Together. Each of us is paying her own share.
MELLERSH	(*aghast*) Paying?! How much?
LOTTY	That, Mellersh . . . I'm afraid . . . is really not at all your affair. (*She gasps and covers her mouth.* MELLERSH'S *jaw drops.*) It came out of my dress allowance. My nest egg. I know you have every reason to be angry and hurt, Mellersh, but I hope you won't and will forgive me instead. This holiday has meant everything to me. Look at me! I've been translated!
MELLERSH	Trans . . . ?
LOTTY	That's why I wanted you here. To be translated with me!
MELLERSH	You know my feelings about secrets, Charlotte!
LOTTY	I know, Mellersh.

MELLERSH   Secrets are like . . .

LOTTY   Rust.

MELLERSH   Yes!

LOTTY   (*shouting*) BUT LOOK AT ME! (*He looks, at
              last.*) I'm not a bit rusty, now, am I?

              (*She kisses him passionately. He is left
              breathless, blushing, grinning.*)

MELLERSH   Well! (*Shudders, turns away.*) If I have made
              my point, then . . . I would very much like a hot
              bath.

LOTTY   (*beaming*) Yes, Mellersh, of course. Costanza!

MELLERSH   Exactly what is it I'm to be translated into,
              Charlotte?

LOTTY   Oh, you'll see, Mellersh. You'll see. (COSTANZA
              enters from the villa.)

COSTANZA   (*wearily*) Sì, Signora?

LOTTY   Ah, Costanza. Signore Wilton . . . (*Smiling.*) . . .
              my husband, Costanza . . . Signore Wilton
              wants a hot bath. Bath.

              (COSTANZA *stares blankly.*)

MELLERSH   The Italian for bath is "bag-no," my dear.
              Bag-no. Here, let me attend to it. (*His Italian is
              comically overdramatic and poorly
              pronounced.*) Io vo-gli-o un bag-no cal-do. *[I
              would like a hot bath.]* (COSTANZA *continues
              to stare.*) Are you certain that she understands
              Italian?

LOTTY   Try again, Mellersh.

MELLERSH   Io . . . vo-gli-o . . . un . . . bag-no cal-do . . .
              Bag-no! Bath! (*He mimes washing, drying.*)
              Bag-no! (COSTANZA *bursts out in laughter.*)

COSTANZA   (*understanding*) Ah! Il Signore vorrebbe un
                bagno caldo!

MELLERSH   Precisely. I think.

COSTANZA   (*laughing, mimicking* MELLERSH'S
                pronounciation and mime) Bag-no cal-do! Un
                momento, Signore. *[One moment.]* (*She exits
                into the villa, laughing.*) Santa Maria!

LOTTY   (*applauding*) Bravo! Bravo!

MELLERSH   (*bowing playfully*) Grat-zee, grat-zee. (*Sighs,
                smiles, looks around.*) This is a beautiful place,
                Charlotte.

LOTTY   Oh, I knew you'd like it!

MELLERSH   But I want to speak to you about the company
                you're keeping.

LOTTY   Well, I assure you, Mellersh . . .

MELLERSH   Lady Caroline Bramble? Really, Charlotte.

LOTTY   Well, I . . .

MELLERSH   You've been very clever, my dear!

LOTTY   Clever?

MELLERSH   I have planned precisely what I should say.

LOTTY   Oh, but you mustn't disturb Lady Caroline.

MELLERSH   I shall be the soul of discretion.

LOTTY   This isn't a business trip, Mellersh.

MELLERSH   No, but . . .

LOTTY   Mellersh!

(COSTANZA *enters with a towel and bath brush.*)

COSTANZA   Bagno pronto, Signore. *[The bath is ready, sir.]*

LOTTY   I'll prepare your things. (*She gets his bag, leaves his hat.*)

MELLERSH   Thank you.

LOTTY   And be careful with the bath, Mellersh. It's very old. You mustn't turn the fire on until . . .

MELLERSH   (*impatiently*) Thank you, Charlotte. (LOTTY *exits.* MELLERSH *starts for the villa, but* COSTANZA *blocks the entrance.*) Bag-no pronto, you say?

COSTANZA   Bagno pronto.

MELLERSH   Very well, then. Thank you. Grat-zee.

COSTANZA   Il bagno è molto vecchio è pericoloso, Signore. *[The bath is very old and dangerous, sir.]*

MELLERSH   Pericoloso?

COSTANZA   (*nodding*) Sì. Bagno pericoloso. (MELLERSH *thinks, huffs, takes out his phrase book, thumbs through it.* COSTANZA *enunciates dramatically.*) Pe - ri - co - lo . . .

MELLERSH   Yes, yes. Pericoloso. (*Finds it.*) Dangerous. Dangerous? A bath?

COSTANZA   Sì. Bagno "booma!"

MELLERSH   Bag-no booma? Good Heavens, I'm a big boy, thank you very much. I can surely take care of myself in a bath.

COSTANZA   (*emphatically*) No, no! Bagno "booma," Signore! Deve stare molto attento! *[You must be very careful.]*

MELLERSH	Very well, bag-no booma, bag-no booma. (*He snatches the towel and brush.*) Now, shoo! Go on! (COSTANZA *scurries onto the terrace.*) Gratzee, Sig-norina. (*He enters the villa.*)
COSTANZA	(*curtsying sarcastically*) "Sig-norina!" (*She huffs, bites her knuckle, clears the tea service, muttering.* LOTTY *enters from the villa, looking for* MELLERSH'S *hat.*)
LOTTY	(*aglow*) Oh, Costanza. Paradiso, Costanza. Paradiso!
COSTANZA	(*humoring her*) Sì, sì, Signora. Paradiso. (*Under her breath.*) Inferno! *[Hell!]*
	(CAROLINE *enters from the villa, dressed for dinner, looking for* FREDERICK.)
LOTTY	Caroline! You are beautiful!
CAROLINE	Have you seen a man?
LOTTY	It's Mellersh! He's arrived!
CAROLINE	Oh, Lotty, good!
LOTTY	It's just as I saw it! But look here. Don't pay Mellersh any mind if he asks you a lot of questions.
CAROLINE	Questions?
LOTTY	With Mellersh, it's best to just say "marvelous," and leave it at that.
CAROLINE	I really am happy for you.
LOTTY	Thank you, Caroline! I can't wait for you to meet him! I'm about to burst!
	(*There is an explosion from within the villa, followed by a pained wail. Clouds of steam*

pour forth. MELLERSH *runs out clad only in a small towel. The ladies stand, stunned, unnoticed.*)

MELLERSH   Damn that bath!

COSTANZA   Bagno pericoloso! Bagno "booma!"

             (MELLERSH *spins, fumbles.*)

MELLERSH   (*to* COSTANZA) Woman!

LOTTY   Mellersh! (*He spins.*)

MELLERSH   Charlotte!

LOTTY   This is most inappropriate, Mellersh.

MELLERSH   I could say as much!

CAROLINE   (*with great formality*) I don't believe we've met.

MELLERSH   (*spinning, aghast*) Ah! Ha! No! No . . . no, we haven't. I . . . I'm afraid I used unpardonable language.

CAROLINE   (*trying not to laugh*) I thought it most appropriate. (*Lifting her hand, making the most of it.*) Lady Caroline Bramble.

MELLERSH   (*smiling weakly at her hand*) How do you do? (*Clears his throat, launches into what he had prepared, as if nothing were wrong.*) I had so been looking forward to our meeting. Mellersh Wilton, family soli . . . (*He attempts to extend his hand, but the towel slips.*)

COSTANZA   Ah!

MELLERSH   Oh!

             (MRS GRAVES *enters from the villa.*)

MRS GRAVES	(*gasping, catching an eyeful*) Oh!
MELLERSH	(*surrounded*) Good God!
CAROLINE	Mr Wilton, may I introduce Mrs Clayton Graves.
MRS GRAVES	The pleasure is all mine!
LOTTY	Now you've met nearly everyone, Mellersh!
MELLERSH	How fortunate. (*To* MRS GRAVES.) How do you do?

(*His towel slips again, exposing his backside. The ladies gasp, smiling.* COSTANZA *quickly covers* MELLERSH *with his hat.*)

COSTANZA	Signore. (*He takes the hat.*)
MELLERSH	Grat-zee. (*He covers himself haphazardly with the hat and towel. The ladies can barely contain their laughter.*) Well . . . well, this has been nice, but . . . but you . . . you . . . you will . . . perhaps another time would be . . .

(*With sudden formality, placing his hat on his head, bowing.*) Excuse me, ladies. (*He bolts into the villa. The ladies laugh.* WILDING *runs from the villa.*)

WILDING	Ladies, ladies. I am sorry. I should have tended to that heater immediately.
MRS GRAVES	"In the flesh," indeed, Mrs Wilton!

(ROSE *and* FREDERICK *run from the villa, straightening themselves.*)

ROSE	Lotty? What on earth?
LOTTY	Oh, it was only Mellersh, Rose.

CAROLINE   (*to* FREDERICK) There you are! (FREDERICK *clutches* ROSE.)

LOTTY   He's arrived!

WILDING   I suppose I had better make some introductions. Mrs Graves, Mrs Wilton, Lady Caroline, allow me to introduce Mrs Arnott's . . . *Mister* Arnott.

(FREDERICK *smiles helplessly.*)

ROSE   Say hello, Frederick.

FREDERICK   (*managing only a weak squeak*) Hello!

MRS GRAVES   (*knowingly*) You look flushed, my boy. One mustn't get too much sun too soon. Isn't that right, Lady Caroline?

(CAROLINE *is frozen. She looks at* ROSE, *who is beaming. She looks at* FREDERICK.)

CAROLINE   (*with complete grace*) Yes, Mr Arnott. We must find you a hat.

(*The sound of piano music, Albéniz's "Suite Española No 1 – Granada." Lights down.*)

Scene Four

Lights up on the terrace, later that evening. Deep blue moonlight. CAROLINE *stands looking out into the garden. Music floats from the villa.* LOTTY *enters from the villa, dressed for dinner.*

LOTTY   There you are. We're having a lovely time inside. What's the matter, Caroline?

(CAROLINE *gathers herself.*)

CAROLINE   (*lost*) I was looking for ghosts.

(LOTTY *thinks, looks out.*)

LOTTY	They're everywhere, aren't they.
CAROLINE	Yes.
LOTTY	Mr Wilding was asking after you.
CAROLINE	Mr Wilding is very charming. As is your Mr Wilton.
LOTTY	Thank you, Caroline. I should have never gotten him started on that piano, though.
CAROLINE	He plays beautifully.
LOTTY	He does, doesn't he!
CAROLINE	Did you see the full moon?
LOTTY	Somehow everything seems full tonight.
CAROLINE	It's love.
LOTTY	I suppose it is.
CAROLINE	The whole place reeks of it. I'll be leaving tomorrow, Lotty.
LOTTY	No, Caroline.

(ROSE *enters from the villa, dressed for dinner.*)

ROSE	Ladies, there's coffee if you'd like. Oh! A full moon! Beautiful!
CAROLINE	(*warming*) It must be a great comfort to be so adored, Mrs Arnott.
ROSE	Oh?
CAROLINE	You and your husband have been making eyes all evening.

ROSE   (*glowing*) We have, haven't we? It's been so
                long since Frederick has read his poetry.

LOTTY   It's wonderful, Rose.

ROSE   Even Mrs Graves thought so!

CAROLINE   (*genuinely*) I really am so happy for you, Rose.

LOTTY   Caroline is lonely, Rose.

CAROLINE   Lotty!

LOTTY   I hadn't seen it until now, but look.

                (ROSE *looks.*)

ROSE   We were sisters all along then, Caroline.

                (FREDERICK *enters from the villa, dressed for
                dinner.*)

FREDERICK   Is the party moving out here now?

LOTTY   Just admiring the view, Mr Arnott.

FREDERICK   Ah!

ROSE   I'm surprised Mrs Graves let you away.

LOTTY   Your poetry is lovely.

FREDERICK   Really?

LOTTY   Yes.

FREDERICK   No.

ROSE   (*going to him*) Don't be modest, Frederick.

FREDERICK   It's wonderful to see you like this, Rose.

ROSE   You as well. (*They kiss.*)

CAROLINE   You are a very lucky man, "Mr Arnott."

FREDERICK   Thank you, "Lady Caroline."

CAROLINE   Rose, you should show your husband the lower garden. In the moonlight it will be extraordinary.

LOTTY   Yes!

ROSE   Would you like to, Frederick?

FREDERICK   Very much.

ROSE   Very well. (*They walk toward the garden, stop.*) Lotty, tomorrow you must take Caroline boating.

LOTTY   Well, of course!

CAROLINE   No, I don't think . . .

ROSE   You'll like that, Caroline. I see it! (*The ladies smile.* ROSE *salutes.*) All'Italia!

LOTTY   All' Italia, Rose!

CAROLINE   All'Italia! (ROSE *and* FREDERICK *exit into the garden.* LOTTY *and* CAROLINE *watch after them, then look out.*) Is this really an enchanted place, Lotty?

LOTTY   Perhaps. You'll have to stay and find out.

                (*The piano has stopped, followed by soft applause and laughter from within the villa.* MRS GRAVES *enters from the villa arm-in-arm with* MELLERSH *and* WILDING. *They are dressed for dinner and carry filled aperitif glasses.*)

MRS GRAVES   Well, I'm not sure London would be ready for Costanza's steak and kidney pie, but for a first effort I thought it exceptional. (*She sees* LOTTY *and* CAROLINE.) Look, gentlemen. Sirens!

MELLERSH	You know, you might find this a bit fantastic, but the one bears a striking resemblance to my wife!
LOTTY	(*smiling coyly*) Mellersh!
	(*She goes to him.* WILDING *goes to* CAROLINE.)
WILDING	Lady Caroline. We've hardly heard a word from you all night. You aren't feeling ill again, I hope.
CAROLINE	Only thinking.
MRS GRAVES	Lady Caroline is fond of thinking, Mr Wilding.
CAROLINE	I was thinking what a wonderful host you've been, Mr Wilding.
LOTTY	Yes.
MELLERSH	We should have proposed a toast to you at dinner.
MRS GRAVES	(*to* WILDING) Is there nothing that will convince you to stay with us a while longer?
WILDING	But I've already packed my things, so that Mr Wilton may have the spare room tonight.
MELLERSH	The spare room?
LOTTY	Oh . . . oh, no, Mr Wilding. Mr Wilton shall share my room, of course.
WILDING	Well, then, I would be honored.
MELLERSH	(*under his breath*) The spare room, Charlotte?
LOTTY	What of Kate Lumley, Mrs Graves? Have you written?
MRS GRAVES	Kate Lumley? Oh, no, no. What Kate Lumley would make of macaroni alone I can but

wonder. (*Thinks.*) Mr Wilding, have you told Lady Caroline the story of the acacia?

WILDING   Well, no.

LOTTY   It's a lovely story, Caroline.

MRS GRAVES   Perhaps you could show her the tree itself.

WILDING   I would like that very much.

               (CAROLINE *smiles.*)

CAROLINE   As would I.

WILDING   Well, right then. I'll get your stick, Mrs Graves.

MRS GRAVES   No, no. I've been without my stick all night. I'm not even sure where I left it. Go on now.

WILDING   Very well. (*Goes to* CAROLINE.) I'm afraid I've been remiss in my duties as host, Lady Caroline. I've been here two days now and I scarcely know a thing about you.

CAROLINE   You must not read the newspapers, Mr Wilding.

WILDING   No. I don't.

CAROLINE   Well, you should. (*She looks at* LOTTY.) You never know what you'll find.

               (WILDING *and* CAROLINE *exit into the garden.* MRS GRAVES *watches after them proudly.*)

MRS GRAVES   There. That's better.

LOTTY   Mrs Graves, perhaps you would read to us from the works of some of your great friends.

MELLERSH   Yes.

MRS GRAVES	Somehow I'm not interested in hearing from my great friends tonight. They always say the same things, don't they?
MELLERSH	But surely their wisdom . . .
LOTTY	And beauty . . .
MRS GRAVES	Yes. Yes. They are. Wise and beautiful. And it would be great folly to ever forget them. But they have one disadvantage. They're dead. If nothing else, at least we all do share the luxury of promise.

(COSTANZA *enters from the villa, dressed in* MRS GRAVES's *costume from Act Two, Scene One, including hat. She carries a bowl of shelled nuts.*)

COSTANZA	(*regally*) "Thee nuts."
LOTTY	Costanza!
MELLERSH	Meravigliosa!

(COSTANZA *bursts out in embarrassed giggles, regains her composure.* MRS GRAVES *goes to her.*)

MRS GRAVES	Getting her into these things of mine was like getting a cat into a sack. And she's shelled the nuts! Took all the fun out of it. Mr Wilton, could I charm you to the piano once more before I retire?
MELLERSH	Nothing would please me more.
MRS GRAVES	I shall be waiting, then. (*Starts to exit into the villa, stops.*) Oh, and both of you please be prompt for breakfa . . .

(COSTANZA *raises her hand.*)

COSTANZA	Eh!

MRS GRAVES   (*begrudgingly*) . . . for "colazione."

COSTANZA   (*proudly, to* LOTTY *and* MELLERSH) Marvelous!

                  (MRS GRAVES *and* COSTANZA *exit. A quiet moment.*)

LOTTY   What an enchanted night, Mellersh.

MELLERSH   It has indeed been quite nice, my dear. Have you been to our room this evening?

LOTTY   Not since dinner. Why?

MELLERSH   Someone has decorated it from floor to ceiling with flowers.

LOTTY   Really?

MELLERSH   Gave me quite a fright. (LOTTY *smiles, looks out into the garden.*)

LOTTY   Mellersh! Look!

MELLERSH   (*looking out*) What?

LOTTY   There! The Roses are lovemaking.

MELLERSH   The "Roses"?

LOTTY   The Arnotts. Is Mrs Arnott familiar to you, Mellersh?

MELLERSH   Mrs Arnott? No.

LOTTY   From church. She's our disappointed Madonna.

MELLERSH   Is she? Well, fancy. I don't recall her being so attractive.

LOTTY   She's bloomed again. And there go the Carolines!

MELLERSH   Really, Charlotte.

LOTTY   Very well, Mellersh. The Wildings, then. And
                I'd wager we'll find Mrs Graves' stick planted
                somewhere in the garden.

MELLERSH   Planted?

LOTTY   I'm sorry, Mellersh, but I see it. (MELLERSH
                opens his mouth to object. LOTTY *raises her
                hand, confidently.*) Case closed, Mellersh.

MELLERSH   (*softly*) I thought I'd lost you, my dear.

LOTTY   Sometimes one just has to step back a bit. Your
                words, Mellersh.

MELLERSH   (*surprised, pleasantly*) Really?

LOTTY   (*in full glory*) It's just a shame this all has to
                end. What could possibly follow such an
                enchanted April?

MELLERSH   I should think . . . an enchanted May! (LOTTY
                *beams, turns and kisses him fully. They are
                silent for a moment. Softly.*) I should go see to
                Mrs Graves. (*He kisses* LOTTY, *starts to exit,
                stops.*) Come in soon.

                (*He smiles and exits into the villa.* LOTTY *looks
                after him, hugs herself, takes it all in.
                Albéniz's "Granada" resumes. Finally, to us,
                completely enchanted.*)

LOTTY   "To those who appreciate wisteria and
                sunshine . . . " (*Sighs.*) Not long after that
                evening, the wisteria at San Salvatore gave
                way, and, though a loss, the castle now
                dressed itself in triumphant white. There were
                white stocks and white pinks and white banksia
                roses, syringa and jessamine, and above all,
                the crowning glory of Mr Wilding's acacia. A
                season had passed, and would pass again. And
                what I see now is that, enchantment aside,

what had really been handed down that month
was . . . (*Sincerely.*) . . . a lesson in gardening.

The wisteria would return the following April.
We all would, in fact. And there would be a
wedding, and a new child. And Kate Lumley.
But that first April we had only just planted our
futures.

And on our final day, as we reached the bottom
of the hill and passed through the castle's
gates, a great warm wind blew through and
against our backs, as if to blow away our
befores forever, now that our afters had begun.

And with the wind came all the scents of San
Salvatore . . . the gardens and the sea,
cinnamon and macaroni. And dancing among
them, white blossoms! Breaking free!

(*White petals start to fall. She looks up,
beaming, raises her arms skyward.*)

Falling . . . like rain!

(*The lights fade as* LOTTY *reaches higher
through the falling petals. End of Play.*)

PROPERTY LIST

London Times (Rose, Lotty, Caroline)
Scissors, mirror, towel (Mellersh)
Monocle (Mellersh)
Book and pen (Frederick)
Gloves (Lotty)
Bowl of nuts, nutcracker (Mrs Graves)
Photographs, postcard (Wilding)
Envelope (Lotty)
Tea service (Wilding)
Dessert, napkin (Mellersh)
Billfold with money (Frederick)
Italian phrase book (Rose)
Travel bags (Rose *and* Lotty)
Beans, bowl (Costanza)
Book (Caroline)
Pitcher (Mrs Graves)
Bell (Mrs Graves)
Cards (Mrs Graves)
Pillow (Caroline)
Tea tray, bowl of nuts (Costanza)
Towels
Parasols (Mrs Graves, Rose)
Flowers (Lotty)
Flask (Caroline)
Bottle of castor oil (Mrs Graves)
Telegram (Costanza, Lotty)
Bag of nuts (Wilding)
Canvas and easel (Wilding)
Tea tray with biscuits (Costanza)
Packages (Lotty *and* Mrs Graves)
Card (Costanza)
Travel bag, hat, coat, phrase book (Mellersh)
Towel (Mellersh)
Filled aperitif glasses (Mellersh, Wilding *and* Mrs Graves)

PROPERTY LIST (Cont.)

Bowl of nuts (COSTANZA)
White petals

SOUND EFFECTS

Thunder
Rain
Train whistle
Train in motion
Church bell
Bell
Explosion
Albéniz's "Suite Española No 1 – Granada"